I LOVE YOU—NOW HUSH

Also by Melinda Rainey Thompson:

SWAG: Southern Women Aging Gracefully (2006)
The SWAG Life (2007)

I LOVE YOU—NOW HUSH

by *Melinda Rainey Thompson*
& Morgan Murphy

JOHN F. BLAIR, PUBLISHER
Winston-Salem, North Carolina

John F. Blair, Publisher
1406 Plaza Drive
Winston-Salem, NC 27103
www.blairpub.com

First Printing 2010

Manufactured in the United States of America

Cover illustration copyright © 2009 by James Bennett

Design by Angela Harwood

Library of Congress Cataloging-in-Publication Data:

Thompson, Melinda Rainey, 1963-
  I love you-now hush / by Melinda Rainey Thompson & Morgan Murphy.
    p. cm.
    ISBN 978-0-89587-378-1 (pbk. : alk. paper) 1. Women--Humor. 2. Man-woman relationships--Humor. 3. Men--Humor. 4. Interpersonal relations--Humor. I. Murphy, Morgan. II. Title.
  PN6231.W6T47 2009
  306.702'07--dc22

                                    2009039457

To my parents, with thanks for giving me a great start in life. I hope my children say nice things about me one day, too.

Melinda

To all the women in my life, Southern or otherwise

Morgan

Contents

Preface   xi
Acknowledgments   xv

Part I
Yes, Dear

Chapter One: Putting It All Together
Melinda: Read the Instructions   5
Excuses Men Make for Not Reading the Instructions   12
Morgan: Just Do It   13
You Know You're in Trouble When   17

Chapter Two: Keeping House
Melinda: From Maiden to Maid   21
The Shocking List of Excuses Men Make to Avoid Housework   27
Morgan: Housekeeping   29
Secrets Men Know about Housekeeping   34

Chapter Three: Getting Around
Melinda: I Can't Get There from Here   37
Morgan: Lost   43
What to Say When She Says, "We're Lost"   47

Chapter Four: On the Prowl
Melinda: A Shopping Philosophy   51
A List of Hard-to-Find Items   56
Morgan: You Need a Retail Therapist   57

Chapter Five: What the #*$&?
Melinda: Watch Your Mouth   63
The Polite Way to Curse   68
Morgan: I Swear   70
How to Upbraid a Person   75

Chapter Six: Southern Semantics
Melinda: Fine with Me   79
Morgan: Decoding Southern Women   84

Chapter Seven: Hoarding
Melinda: Save That for Me   89
Ten Things Every Woman Saves   95
Morgan: A Penny Saved Is a Cent   96

Chapter Eight: That Twinkle in Your Eye
Melinda: All That Glitters   103
Morgan: Shiny Things   107

Chapter Nine: Valentine's Day
Melinda: Construction-Paper Hearts   113
Morgan: The Big V   118

**Part II
You Say, "Tomato";
I Say, "Where's the Lettuce and the Bacon?"**

Chapter Ten: Romancing the South
Melinda: One Romantic Gesture   127
How to Romance a Southern Woman   132
Morgan: Romance for Less   134
How to Romance Any Southern Male   138

Chapter Eleven: Surviving Crash Diets
Melinda: Diet Drama   141
Morgan: Suck It In   146
Worth Gaining a Few   150

Chapter Twelve: Vanity Unfair
Melinda: Brace Yourself   153
Morgan: Hair of the Man   159

Chapter Thirteen: Fa So La Ti Da
Melinda: Tips from a Soprano   165
Morgan: Bass Observations   170

Chapter Fourteen: Gadgets and Gizmos
Melinda: New and Improved   177
Inventions I Need ASAP   182
Morgan: Man's Four Phases of Technology   183

Chapter Fifteen: Embrace Your Inner Foodie
Melinda: Chocolate, My One True Love   189
How to Use Chocolate for Good   195
Morgan: Eat, Drink, and Be Manly   197
Rules for Eating Out   202

Chapter Sixteen: The Buck Stops Here
Melinda: Money Matters   205
Morgan: It's Not Easy Being Green   209

Chapter Seventeen: The Not-So-Great Outdoors
Melinda: Yard Work Is for Men   217
Morgan: A Controlled Burn   223
How to Look and Sound Like a Pro in the Garden   229

Chapter Eighteen: You Are What You Wear
Melinda: All Dressed Up   233
Dress-Up Clues   239
Morgan: Invasion of the Suit Snatchers   241
Fashion Disasters   246

Preface

This book was all my idea. You need to know that. If you like it, you can thank me by buying one copy for yourself and another one for a friend. If you don't like it, well, you can blame my coauthor, Morgan Murphy, a well-mannered Southern gentlemen, a man who is perfectly willing to fall on his sword for me. I just love chivalry. Don't you?

It is hard for me to confess this again, but this book, my third, was another accident. I'd like to say that it was a well-thought-out plan from its conception, but that would be a lie. I sold my first book, *SWAG: Southern Women Aging Gracefully*, after writing and publishing a newsletter, *The SWAG Letter*, for five years. While I was waiting for my first book's release, I kept writing, and my second book, *The SWAG Life*, crept up on me.

I thought I'd gotten that business out of my system, but regular life down here in Alabama continues to tempt me to write about it. You just would not believe. Every single day something happens that I can't wait to describe for you in delicious detail. It wasn't long before new chapters began to leak out of my fingertips. My husband and children seemed resigned, if not thrilled, by the sight of me hunched over my laptop. (Of course, these same ungrateful wretches are plenty excited when Mom earns extra cash for eating out, football tickets, or a new fuel pump for the car. Okay, nobody was really excited about the fuel pump, but thank goodness I had a speaking fee to cover its demise.)

Book number three started out full throttle. For the first six months, I knew exactly where it was going, and I could see the chapter highway in front of me lit up like the Talladega raceway. That was delightful. I had a good plan, a schedule, and complete control of everything in my writing orbit. Life was good. Then, something happened, something completely unexpected, something that has never happened to me in all the years I have been writing: I got stuck. I was halfway through this book when, all of a sudden, I could not visualize it anymore as a finished product. I did not like it one bit. I wailed. I cried. I threw myself across my bed and pitched a fit. I lolled on my porch swing. I took long bubble baths for inspiration. I whined to my girlfriends on the telephone. No matter what I tried, I could not force myself to finish this book. I leaned back on the hind legs of my desk chair and stared blankly at my computer screen. What could it mean?

I am a busy woman. I don't have the time or the temperament for writing angst or other self-indulgent nonsense. I had to figure out what was wrong. Eventually, I had a writing epiphany—not a Kate Chopin epiphany, which would have resulted in me finally sliding both feet off the ledge and jumping—a practical, down-to-earth, helpful epiphany. Really, it was more like a "Eureka!" moment that came to me in the middle of the night. I threw off the bedcovers, crawled over my long-suffering husband, jumped out of bed, fired up my computer, and began writing again in an inspired frenzy.

I'd been going about this book all wrong. This book needed another voice, a balancing counterpoint, the "he said" to my "she said." What this book needed was Morgan Murphy. I knew it like when you take a pound cake out of the oven and know it is going to be perfect before you slice into it. From that moment on, I cold-bloodedly set about lassoing my coauthor.

I've known Morgan for years. He was my all-time favorite student at Birmingham-Southern College. He writes beautifully. He should. I taught him. He is one of the funniest men I have ever met. He makes me laugh so hard I think I am going to throw up. Not many people do that. He is grand fun. I can't wait to introduce him to you on our book tour. We'll be doing speaking events together, too. You won't be able to resist him. I guarantee it.

I was determined to sign him on to this project. I planned my campaign carefully. I filled a legal pad with all the reasons why Morgan should agree to do exactly what I wanted. If he refused, I had a backup plan to sell his wife, Amy, on the idea. I called him on his cell phone to tell him I needed to talk to him. I know full well that Southern men are programmed to respond unconditionally to a Southern woman who needs something they can provide. I asked him how soon he could drop by. "How about ten minutes?" he asked. He was already in his car. That right there is one of the many reasons I love men like Morgan. He knew instinctively that although I said I wanted to see him as soon as conveniently possible, I really meant "in ten minutes."

While driving to my house and talking to me on his cell phone, Morgan asked, "What do you want?"

I looked down at my legal pad, took a deep breath, and decided to lay my cards on the table: "I want you to write a book with me, Morgan. Actually, I'm already halfway through with the book. You have some catching up to do. I am completely confident that you can do it."

He didn't hesitate. "I don't have to think about that," Morgan said. "I'll do it."

From that moment on, the book was clear in my mind's eye again. I knew exactly what it should look like, sound like, and, hopefully, sell like. I hope you like it. I hope you find your own life in these pages and laugh out loud. That is, after all, why we wrote it.

Melinda Rainey Thompson

When a Southern woman asks a Southern gentleman to do something, he does it. Especially when that woman possesses the fiery intellect and somewhat frightening verbal skills of Melinda Rainey Thompson.

I tell stories. I've always told stories. Before *Vanity Fair*, *Forbes*, *Esquire*, and *Southern Living*, there was English 101 at Birmingham-Southern College. The professor, my coauthor, taught a riveting class full of witty asides, hilarious anecdotes, and some truly brilliant advice that helped me eventually become an executive editor at the world's largest publishing company.

As a professor, Melinda offered many rules, regulations, and notes on grammar in one handy, laminated "cheat sheet." She stood on a chair one day and made us all promise to take it with us everywhere, even to our *graves* (insert trademark Melinda drama here). While I think I've broken most of the rules, I've always kept a copy of her editing remarks in my desk drawer, right next to the booze and the tobacco.

All of this is to say that were it not for Melinda Thompson, I might never have entered the cutthroat, penniless, finicky, ephemeral, and unpredictable world of magazine journalism. I might have tried my hand at high finance or plumbing and made millions. I could have gone into politics and told even bigger whoppers than you'll find in my chapters of this book.

Read. Laugh. Share. And if you enjoy what you find here, know that I learned it from the best. And if you don't like it, consider the source.

Morgan Murphy

Acknowledgments

First of all, thanks to my friend and coauthor, Morgan Murphy, for agreeing without hesitation to write his first book with me, even though his life was already crammed full. In my experience, writing a book is never convenient.

As always, thanks to the staff at John F. Blair, Publisher. No writer could ask for a better relationship than I have with you. I count each of you as a blessing. Thanks, especially, to Carolyn Sakowski for signing on to this project when it was just an idea and trusting me to deliver it. To my fabulously talented, mind-reader editor, Angela Harwood, thanks for doing what you always do: take a book and make it better.

To my sweet friends, thanks for turning out for book signings, for helping me find where I'm supposed to be, for reading random chapters, and for recommending my books to your friends. Southern women like you are a word-of-mouth force to be reckoned with. Thanks, this time, especially to: Phyllis, Vivian, Tricia, Laura, Whitney, Barbara, Vera, and all the members of St. Stephen's choir.

Thanks to SIBA (Southeastern Independent Booksellers Association) and all the booksellers who welcome me into their stores and take the time to hand sell my books all through the year.

Thanks to my children for being good sports about appearing in my pages, and to my husband and mother, who both keep my other jobs humming so that I can do the writing work I love.

My deepest, most heartfelt thanks go to *SWAG* readers everywhere for showing up at speaking events, standing in line at book signings, and telling me your stories. I remember every single one of you, and you're right—I am writing about your life, too!

Melinda

My eccentric and flamboyant former editors taught me the craft of writing. They also gave me a career and paid me to tell stories for fifteen years. Long may their glossy pages shimmer.

My teachers labored mightily to squash some sense into me, in part because I was always off on some harangue or telling jokes in the corner. One of them, turned coauthor, holds more faith in my abilities than perhaps is wise, but God love her for it. There's no greater accolade than the supportive words and genuine encouragement of a favorite teacher. Thank you, Melinda.

My family taught me the love of storytelling. The matriarchs: Mama, Grandmama, Helen—when someone says "lady," I think of each of you. The baby sisters: Marissa, Meredith, and Lauren—no brother could ask for better. Thank you, Guy and Grandaddy, for keeping generations of stories on hand to relay at a moment's notice. Thank you, Daddy, for being the seersuckered gentlemen who taught me how to tell those stories and how to never laugh at your own jokes, how you can't win if you don't try, and for silently showing me the meaning of duty to one's family.

My first book publisher, John F. Blair, gave me a shot in a longer format. I'm grateful to Angela Harwood and Carolyn Sakowski for their faith.

My wife, Mrs. Murphy, never stopped saying "You can do it." I thank her for her love and support.

Morgan

PART I
Yes, Dear

Chapter 1

Putting It All Together

Read the Instructions

The men in my life seem philosophically opposed to reading the instructions before beginning a do-it-yourself project. They see it as a sign of weakness, apparently, a threat to their manly characters or something. Men act like reading the instructions is cheating or unsportsmanlike, at the very least, and possibly against their religions. I cannot fathom why this is true. It makes no sense. Obviously, one does need the instructions if the manufacturer paid someone to write them—in English, Spanish, Portuguese, French, German, and Japanese. Do men think the manufacturer went to all that trouble just for the fun of it? Surely not.

At first, I assumed that only my husband passed on reading the instructions, but I've done some research (okay, I emailed my girlfriends and asked about their experiences), and this lack of instruction reading is as common as nail fungus. I first encountered it shortly after I got married. (Don't you love how we say we "got married" down here? It's like we've been infected by something beyond our control, as in, "The baby got croup, so I took her to the pediatrician.") My husband

and I bought our first do-it-yourself project: bookshelves. This was an appropriate purchase in many ways. We were both in graduate school. The only thing we did together was read. We were flat broke, so the bookshelves were not made by a Swedish craftsman. The finished product looked like something a North Korean assembly-line worker knocked together on his lunch break.

Now that I think about it, the first project a newlywed couple undertakes is almost a rite of passage. I bet you can recall a similar experience. If not, you will be able to imagine this one easily: A young couple heads to Home Depot on a Saturday morning in spring, steaming coffee cups, list, and measuring tape clutched tightly in their eager little fingers, arms around each other's waists in a revolting display of kissy-face enthusiasm that says they love to do everything together. (Thank the Lord we all grew out of that stage fairly quickly. It makes me nauseous just remembering it.) The vision of a completed set of bookshelves, proudly hugging a corner in our first living room and piled high with all of our favorite books, shimmered in our gaga little newlywed eyes. In those days, we really thought the finished product would look like the picture on the box. Was I ever that naïve? I can barely remember those days.

As soon as we returned to our just-married apartment, we both readied ourselves for project time. I tuned in to a public radio station to set the mood. I refilled my coffee mug, changed into an old sweatshirt, found a pencil, and began assembling an assortment of household tools with all the studiousness of a paramedic restocking the ambulance supplies.

That's when I heard it—an inhuman ripping sound from the living room. It sounded exactly like a box being ripped apart by a pack of Arctic wolves.

I immediately darted into the living room and came face to face with my first "men think about stuff differently" marital moment. With one quick look, my bridal eyes were opened to an entirely new landscape. After the parties are over, the thank-you notes are written, and the bride takes off the big, white dress, the marital reality is often shocking. It was clear to me right there in my living room that my husband and I did not think alike—maybe about anything.

I was poised, pencil behind my ear, ready to help my husband carefully unload the giant box from the trunk of the car, with the aid of a hand truck, which I had not yet unearthed from the hall closet. (I thought that a hand truck was a strange housewarming present a few weeks earlier, but, in retrospect, it was an inspired gift that kept on giving over the years.) I was still making PREPARATIONS for our project. In my mind, project time couldn't begin for at least another fifteen minutes. I was still involved in the pregame show.

Our brand-new living room looked like a bomb had gone off in it. I stood frozen in the doorway to take in the devastation like a National Guard soldier surveying flood damage from a helicopter before swooping in to save the residents with a rooftop pickup. The front door to our apartment was standing wide open to thieves and peddlers alike. A neighbor's dog paused at our threshold to sniff with interest the smells emanating from unit 1671-B.

I could see through the doorway that the trunk of the car had also been left gaping. In addition, my husband had obviously not thought it important to remove the keys from the ignition of the car before storming the front door of the apartment like a police officer busting up an illegal gambling ring. I knew this because that annoying, "You forgot your keys!" beeping was still going on about two octaves above middle C. Moving forward, I could see two long gashes in the flower beds lining my sidewalk where, apparently, the giant box of shelves had been dragged willy-nilly through my freshly planted begonias, the first "welcome to our house" flowers I ever planted as a married woman. There seemed to be no end to the insults.

I could see quite easily the path my husband had taken while dragging the big box because the dirt from the flower beds and a few accompanying begonia casualties continued through the wide-open front door and across the carpet to the middle of the living room where the box obviously came to an abrupt halt after colliding with our coffee table. I guessed that all on my own, without being told, because two wedding presents, a Waterford biscuit jar, given to us by my grandmother, and a silver bud vase, given to us by a work colleague we both despised, were knocked over and clinging perilously to the edge of the coffee table.

I was speechless. My husband, on the other hand, had the audacity to look cheerful—excited even.

"Sweetheart, can you drag that empty box out to the street? We won't need it anymore," my husband tossed out over his shoulder in my direction.

Although it seemed impossible, every indication assured me that the man was speaking to me. How in the world had I automatically been cast as the helper in our project?

It was hard to decide what I wanted to be upset about first. I had a number of concerns. Why was my husband wielding a screwdriver in one hand as if he was about to tighten up something on the space shuttle when we barely had the box out of the car? Why were we throwing the box away? Wasn't that a bit precipitous? What if we had to return it? What if we accidentally left something in the box that we needed later? Had my husband double-checked? I doubted it.

That's when I looked inside the box and saw the instruction manual. You guessed it. My new husband, who had just weeks before promised to love and cherish me (I wanted to throw in the traditional "obey" with a new twist, but he wouldn't go for it.), was THROWING AWAY the directions.

"Did you know the directions are *still in here*?" I squealed at the freak I had so hastily and recently wed.

"Oh, I don't need those," he said. "This is going to be a piece of cake to put together."

That statement right there was a watershed in our marriage. I was just too young and inexperienced to realize it. It was a signifier of things to come. To this day, my husband never needs directions. Let me clarify that: he never *thinks* he needs directions. He certainly does not want to read the directions beforehand. If worse comes to worse, and he has to give them a look-see later, then he'll do that right after throwing something in a fit of temper.

My husband opens packaging with his teeth; snaps parts off cardboard and plastic; casts aside instructional DVDs, manuals, and diagrams; and rushes right in with his big hands and feet where angels fear to tread. He is not afraid to push buttons just to see what will happen. Try-it-and-see is his favorite game plan. He has confidence that whatever he attempts—even though he has never attempted it before in his whole life nor seen anyone else do it—will be up and running satisfactorily in short order.

As galling as it is for me to have to admit this, he usually pulls it off. I'd like to say that I am a big enough person to be happy for him, but that would be a lie. It makes me mad every single time things work out for him when he's done nothing whatsoever to deserve it. I have been forced to recognize that there might be something to his whole show-of-confidence, admit-no-weakness, and take-no-prisoners approach to projects. He also swears copiously when he puts things together, and I have known him to hit the bar pretty hard when he's in the throes of a project, but I have to admit, in the end, things usually work out well for him. Bully for him.

This success does not change the fact that the way he tackles projects is all wrong. It makes me sick to my stomach to watch him. My blood pressure goes up so high I can feel my face flush. We learned when we tried to wallpaper our first bathroom together that a couple who wallpapers together probably will not stay together for long. We tried wallpapering separate walls; then we tried working in different rooms. Finally, we decided that in the interest of marital harmony, we'd better call in professional paperhangers. Sometimes, it pays to just write a check. That right there is as good a piece of marital advice as you'll get from anyone if you live to be a hundred.

My approach to any project is not just different from my husband's. It's better. I am highly organized. As you might guess, I am very big on preplanning. I approach any project like the nighttime invasion of a foreign country. I do the research. I ask others about their experiences. By the time I purchase supplies, I usually know more about the project than anyone else in this hemisphere. This approach requires lots of talking and sharing of ideas. You can see this is a deal killer for most men.

I wait for a day when the stars are aligned perfectly for my project's success. I read the instruction manual, and I use a highlighter. After I finish reading, I read it again. I'll give you a free tip right here: I compare the directions in other languages. You better believe it. You can count on the French to give the best, most complete directions in *French*—not English. They don't like us much, and messing up an American shelf project is just the kind of thing the French like to do. Finally, I set up my equipment in a pre-staging area and commit to a final battle plan. It is days, weeks sometimes; it could even be another season of the year entirely, before I actually *do* anything.

The problem with my approach, of course, is that it is a wee bit time-consuming. If the kid is shaving before you get the training wheels on his bike, they probably aren't going to do much good. Also, when the directions fail, or some part is missing (do you think they leave out screws on purpose, just to mess with our minds?), or a bit of creative improvisation is called for, I've got nothin'.

I'm afraid to try anything that is not expressly described in the directions. I take those instruction warnings seriously. The scratchy tags are still on my mattresses. The tags say, "Do not remove under penalty of law." I do not fool around with breaking the law. I have a hard enough time trying not to break the law accidentally.

I'd like to remind you that there are flaws with my husband's no-directions-needed approach, too. For one thing, sometimes, he breaks some of my favorite things. Collateral damage is virtually guaranteed. For another, his approach is messy. Occasionally, he hurts himself putting something together. Once or twice, I was afraid that one of the children or an innocent neighbor might get injured, too. My husband once got a sofa stuck in our front doorway. For a while, I thought it was going to have to stay like that until we moved. I'd gotten as far as planning to move the planter by my front door to the back door to dress that entrance up a bit if we were going to have to live with a front door with a couch stuck in it. Another time, he got the television working, which was great. Unfortunately, all the lights on one side of the house went out. It wasn't a good trade-off.

After twenty-one years of marriage, I've learned to live with the different ways my husband and I approach projects. I am wise enough not to say things out loud like, "Why in the world are you doing that? Have you completely lost your mind?" and "Well, what did you think would happen when you did that?" I still *think* them, though.

Excuses Men Make for Not Reading the Instructions

"I left my reading glasses at the office. I'm going to have to go with my gut."

"I'm not reading any foreign instructions."

"I don't need instructions because I saw somebody do this on television last week. It turned out great."

"I'll read the instructions if I can't figure it out on my own."

"I don't need those instructions. All I need is this screwdriver, my drill, and pure muscle."

"My father used to have one just like this. He didn't have any instructions. The know-how is in the blood."

"If I need help, I'll ask somebody down at the hardware store."

"The instructions are in there to keep them from being sued. It's like the 'careful, it's hot' labels on fast-food coffee cups. That is embarrassing for the whole country."

"All I need is this diagram, and I am good to go."

"I have an MBA. I don't need instructions for anything."

"Don't worry about it. I'm practically an expert."

Just Do It

Yes, I see the instructions. No, I do not want to read them.

Believe, if you will, that men irrationally disregard instructions in order to wreak mayhem and destruction upon the women in their lives. Go on with your studying, your analyzing, your boring instruction reading.

For I will be in the backyard, with a perfectly assembled grill, swing set, bike, whatever, while you are still on Step A: "Insert flat handled jig into slide-folded slot 2.B."

"This is not a race," you might say.

On the contrary, dear, it is indeed a race. A race to the finish. A race to the end of the abject misery it is to put together that desk, shelf, or complicated trash can you purchased.

"How do you know that *I* purchased this object in need of assembling?" you're thinking, not without some degree of indignation.

That's an easy one: men don't buy things we don't understand. Really. We hate shopping (see chapter four). So we don't buy things on a whim, on a lark, or because it looked "nice." We buy things because we have done the research, studied it, talked to our buddies about it, and obsessed over it for weeks, sometimes months.

What do you think we men talk about? We don't talk about our *feelings* and *emotions*. Good Lord, no. We talk about stuff:

"My deck is made with a new space-age polymer that wicks moisture . . ."

"That grill has a self-ignition system that will singe a charcoal briquette into gray matter . . ."

"The filter on my pool is made with nanotechnology and can filter urine into potable water . . ."

How do you think we learned all this? We had to study, by damned. Getting an MBA was easier than figuring out the inner workings of my stereo system. The SAT took less prep time than my new SLR Nikon.

And you know what? It's not a burden, a chore, a hideous task. We love studying stuff, taking care of it, bragging to our friends that the stuff they bought is inferior or, better yet, usurping their knowledge of their own stuff with our amazing command of the user's manual. Yes, indeed, we're all like a bunch of overgrown Boy Scouts with the motto, "Be prepared . . . to know the arcane workings of a Dewalt table saw."

And then you come home with a new microwave, with instructions.

Now, all men have a specialty or want to have a specialty. Some guys might actually love microwaves. Those are the electronic guys that know how to program a cable box or reset the diagnostic codes on the family sedan. Other fellows are more of the craftsman types, who like quality and construction, who admire real wood, brass, and copper. They'll spend eighty dollars on a set of wood screws. Then there's the MacGyver man who prides himself on never spending any money but creating elaborate new home contrivances out of chewing gum and old baby food jars.

If your fella is the electronic type, he doesn't *need* to read the instructions. He could program your microwave to take command of a Mars Rover and cook a turkey at the same time.

If your fella isn't the electronic type, he doesn't *want* to read the instructions because they are boring, annoying, and for an appliance he dislikes.

Instructions fall into two categories: incredibly simple or incredibly complicated. There's no middle ground.

For example, here's a common manly purchase: a lawnmower. I needed a mower—I've got about a half-acre of grass, so it's too small for a riding mower but too large for a push mower. So I started talking to friends. My friend Brad recommended a Snapper, telling me it could mulch a steel trash can into confetti. That sounded cool, so I looked online and ended up buying a John Deere with more horsepower than my first car, a mulching blade that could also dice the carrots for Sunday dinner, and enough attachments to outfit the next invasion of North Korea. It's awesome, and my exhaustive research shows it's better than Brad's old Snapper, which is, after all, the point.

It also came in eleven pieces: a handle, four handle bolts, four wheels, a side-discharge adjustment bolt, and a bag. Did I read the instructions? Hell no. Why? Because they're written for people who don't know the working end of a lawnmower.

Take for example, checking the oil in my lawnmower. It couldn't be simpler. There's a big knob on the top of the mower labeled (surprise) "OIL." Yet instruction manuals have to be written for bona-fide idiots, the lowest common denominator, the people who would try to start the mower with their nostrils or something. So "OIL" does not suffice. The manual, written by lawyers, has to *explain* and *qualify* and *warn explicitly.*

These are actual instructions from my mower's manual, which I read for the first time as research for this chapter:

Park mower on level surface and stop engine.

Clean area around dipstick (A).

Remove dipstick and wipe clean.

Install and tighten dipstick.

Remove dipstick.

Check oil level on dipstick. Oil must be between ADD and FULL marks.

If oil level is low, add oil to bring oil level no higher than

FULL mark on dipstick. Do not overfill.

Install and tighten dipstick.

Eight steps! Eight! But wait, there's more. A big disclaimer: "IMPORTANT: Avoid damage! Do not overfill. Overfilling with oil can cause the engine to not start or hard starting. If oil is over the FULL mark on the dipstick, drain oil to reduce oil level in engine."

All this to explain the concept of a *dipstick*, which is such a simple device that in the common vernacular it is slang for *idiot*.

The manual goes on for what seems like four thousand pages. And for what? All you need to know about a mower is pull cord; repeat. And heaven forbid you really need to find any information—you'll have to wade through such gems of wisdom as, "AVOID INJURY! Touching hot surfaces can burn skin," and, "Do not smoke while handling fuel," and my favorite, "For outdoor use only." Shoot, I had planned on mowing down the Oriental rug.

Sadly, my mower manual is one of the good ones, written in America by someone whose first (second or third) language is English. Try one of those instruction pamphlets, printed on see-through Charmin, folded into some kind of origami bird, and written in Korean, Sanskrit, and German. If the product doesn't poke your eyes out, the instructions will.

Instructions to men are like a nuclear weapon or a Hail Mary: only to be used as a last resort. The mower is on fire, the lawn is burning, the blade has come off and is stuck in a tree—then, and only then, do we read the instructions to see where we went wrong. In the event of such an emergency, you don't simply go thumbing through an instruction manual out in the open. Goodness no. You must hide that sucker behind a *Playboy*, read under the cloak of darkness, or run out to the garage to leaf through its mind-numbing pages.

Otherwise, we men might blow the image that we know what we're doing.

You Know You're in Trouble When

The box says, "Some Assembly Required."

You realize "some assembly" means "requires an engineering degree in applied physics."

You are putting together a gift for a child under ten.

You opted to save money and assemble the item yourself rather than pay the store to do it.

It is Christmas Eve.

At 3:00 a.m.

Santa is drunk on eggnog.

Mrs. Claus is furious.

Barbie's Dream Home resembles GI Joe's camp after the war.

休几〉一 凵夕彐

Chapter 2

Keeping House

From Maiden to Maid

Melinda Rainey Thompson

It isn't fair. I don't mean unfair as in, "It's not fair that some women can eat chili-cheese fries every night of the week and wash them down with chocolate milk shakes and never gain an ounce." I mean unfair as in "great social injustice." I'm talking big picture here. On the home front, women do more work than men. You know it's true. It's a proven fact. Don't bother to try and justify it. I don't want to hear it. I don't even care how it came to *be* true. It is what it is, and what it is stinks.

When men unload the dishwasher, fold the laundry, shop for groceries, or scrub the bathtub grout with an old toothbrush, everyone in three counties praises them to the skies for being marvelous helpers. I've actually been told: "Your husband makes the kids' breakfast before he goes to work? Aren't you lucky! The judge is so sweet."

This is true. He is sweet. That's not the point. This kind of praise makes me furious. A friend once asked me, "Is your husband babysitting for you?" "No," I said, "they're his kids, too." She picked right up on my giant-chip-on-the-shoulder response and immediately kicked the conversational can farther down the highway.

I would prefer to be the domestic helper. Who wouldn't? Any chores the helper performs at home, in addition to a regular job in the working world (for which he or she is already highly respected by society, praised by peers, paid cash money, and which earn him or her retirement and health-care benefits), are rewarded with gold stars for effort. Who wants to be in charge of the home front? No glamour there at all. It is not fun to be the one who makes sure the laundry is transferred from the washer to the dryer all day long, cleans out the litter box, changes the filters, remembers to pick up milk, and helps deliver the Girl Scout cookies. But if you are the helper, every single task you perform in addition to the job you are paid for is like extra credit.

Do you know what the job description entails for the stay-at-home person? I'll tell you: everything that has to be done that can't or won't be done by anyone else who lives in the house. Stay-at-home moms have the most jobs of all. I know. I am one. We are like the Statue of Liberty. We should have signs that say, "Send us your tired, your hungry, your feverish, your surly and badly behaved teenage masses. Whatever you've got, we can handle it."

Guess who stays home to meet the plumber, the cable guy, or the exterminator? I bet you the Hershey bar in my sock drawer that it's a woman ninety-nine percent of the time. If there are aging parents to be cared for, guess who handles that? If the school calls to extort six-dozen brownies for the bake sale or chaperones for a sweaty field trip to the African Congo, guess who answers the call? Part of it is our fault, of course, because we respond faster than the state's SWAT team. If there are teenagers in need of chauffeur services, pancakes, dating advice, SAT tutoring, or physical therapy, you'll find a woman answering those needs, too.

Does your dry cleaning need to be picked up from Nova Scotia? There's probably a woman in your life who will find a way to swing by on her way home from work. The church needs a dozen palm fronds for Palm Sunday by lunch tomorrow? No problem. Some resourceful woman will find them. Is your baseball uniform coated in red mud and enough blood to send hound dogs into a tracking frenzy? Did you forget to take it out of your sports bag until midnight but need it by 6:30 a.m.? The Four Seasons Hotel won't launder under those time constraints, but Mom will. Even if your uniform has white pants, a red shirt, and blue socks—which will require three different loads of laundry—Mom will stay up until 3:00 a.m. to wash everything. Don't give it another thought.

Baby threw up in his crib? Somebody stepped in dog poop while jogging? Leave those running shoes by the front door. Mom will eventually quit waiting for you to clean them and do it herself. No need to mention it. Did the cat cough up a hair ball on the dining-room carpet? No need to pause on your way to watch television in the living room. Mom will take care of it.

We all know who ends up doing the most distasteful jobs around the house. Mom. Before my middle child was old enough to speak in complete sentences, he used one word, *mom*, as his personal 911 call. If his brother snatched a toy, he would howl at the top of his lungs: "Mom!" If he was afraid of a dog approaching his stroller for a friendly sniff, he'd yell: "Mom!" If he was thirsty, hot, trapped inside the bathroom, or just a little bored, he'd yell "Mom!" and wait for the cavalry to arrive.

Frankly, I'm tired of the martyr role. I'd like to redistribute the housework among my comrades like a good communist party leader. Maybe it did do some good for well-educated professionals to work in the rice paddies during the Cultural Revolution in China. I'm not saying I would go about things exactly like the Chinese did, but a little taste of Mom's jobs would be good for all the people who live in this house, I think.

I somehow manage the arduous task of blowing my nose and throwing my soiled tissues into one of the many conveniently located trash cans scattered throughout our home. My children, on the other hand, routinely throw their snotty nose rags in the vicinity of a trash can and then rely on Mom to come along behind them, pick up the germy tissues, and throw the suckers away. Since I also regularly use the potty without spraying the toilet seat or surrounding tiles, I don't really think I should have to clean that up either—yet I do. I am way over-educated for my current position. I'm seriously considering other employment options. Honestly, I think I could name my price as a nanny on the open market. Then I could get week-ends off. I'd get paid, too. Imagine that. The more I think about it, the better it sounds. If I worked as a professional house-keeper or nanny, I promise you that women would be fighting hand to hand in the streets to hire me. I could name my price. I'm good.

I don't know who first decided on the distribution of household chores in America, but I have a sneaking suspicion it was a man. He was probably a Calvinist. I'd like to know his name. If I could travel back in time, I'd pay him a little visit and beat the stuffing out of him.

It doesn't matter how many jobs men and women have outside their homes. It doesn't matter if they have children or not. It doesn't matter about education, marital or social sta-tus, or how much money they earn. No matter what variables you insert in the formula, the answer never varies. Women do more housework than men. This reality crosses international, cultural, and religious borders as easily as a cold virus in the jet age. The same stinking thing happens all over the world.

I feel a political moment coming on. I want to talk to my senators (both male—big shockeroo) about the working con-ditions of women on the home front. How is it possible that in households where men and women both have "real" jobs, women still do more work?

Don't even get me started on whether or not I have a real job as a stay-at-home mom. The next person who asks me, "Do you work?"—as if the only work that counts as a real job is in an office somewhere—may just lose a kneecap. I know where the baseball bats are in this house, and I've watched my boys enough to believe I could do some damage. Furthermore, al-though I don't like to think of myself as a violent person, I might enjoy it. I'm mad enough to swing for the fences. In years gone by, when someone asked me, "Do you work?" I'd stumble around an answer with sheepish responses like, "Well, I used to be a teacher. Now, I'm a stay-at-home mom, and I do some writing. . . ." Usually, the questioner totally lost interest by the time I articulated a coherent answer.

Things are different now. When someone asks, "Do you work?" I always look him or her dead in the eyes and say, "Yes, I do. Hard." That's all. If the questioner hangs around long enough after that testy response, and if he or she is stupid enough not to pick up on that do-not-touch-this-subject-with-a-barge-pole hint, I elaborate.

I have worked several jobs society considers real jobs— you know, jobs with a paycheck. None of those jobs was nearly as hard as the job I have now as a stay-at-home mom. I am on call twenty-four hours a day. It's a catchall job, like the super-intendent of a large New York apartment building. As a mom, I routinely perform the work of a: janitor, cook, maid, costume designer, cleaner, nurse, artist-in-residence, driver, prison warden, private investigator, hostage negotiator (it happens), paramedic, physical therapist, bouncer, lifeguard, game war-den, teacher, coach, psychiatrist, career counselor, financier, priest, and confessor.

I'm not unusual. I know many, many women who do the same things every day. Believe me when I tell you that you don't get into this line of work for the money. A few times over the years, another mommy has had the audacity to say to me, out loud: "I don't know how you do that stay-at-home thing. That wasn't for me." "Me either," I always say. "It didn't do my career one bit of good. I did it because I was able to swing it fi-nancially; I'm good at it; and I think it's good for my kids." (You either have the nose to sniff out the plans of sneaky teenagers, or you don't. It's a gift.)

Sadly, the stay-at-home-mom job is often about as intel-lectually stimulating as picking lint off a winter coat. That's how I first started writing. Readers always ask me, "Three chil-dren? How do you have time to write?" I answer truthfully. I don't have time to write. It's not impossible, but it's close. It's as close to impossible as it can be without being impossible. That's the best way I can describe it.

(I have a chapter about parenting in my book, *The SWAG Life*, titled "I Quit." If you are a stay-at-home parent, you need to read it. You'll feel better about yourself after you read about one of my worst parenting days. If you are not a stay-at-home parent, you need to read it to remind yourself why your nanny deserves a Christmas bonus. And if you are a man, stay-at-home parent or not, well, you need to read everything I write. I'm doing everything I can to help you.)

It's hard for me to separate jobs that women do from parenting—whether they have children or not. My jobs as a woman and as a mom overlap. Women's job descriptions are never as clear-cut as men's. They're blurry, connected to one another, other people, and to society as a whole. (Good grief. That sounds preachy. I apologize.) I was not a bit surprised the first time I saw the movie *Snow White*, when Snow White stumbles across a cottage crammed full of seven male dwarves and yet, somehow, she ends up cooking, cleaning, and washing for the whole lot of them. Were you?

The Shocking List of Excuses Men Make to Avoid Housework

"I would love to clean the toilets, but you do it so much better than I ever could. You are a talented woman.
I am so glad I married you."

"The dog made another mess in the living room! I'll clean it up after work, okay? Don't even think about doing it yourself."

"Didn't we clean the bathroom last week?
We hardly ever even use it."

"What mess? It looks clean to me."

"What's the point in straightening up? The kids
are just going to mess it up again."

"My stomach's not feeling that great. I think
I need to take a little nap first."

"I'm planning to vacuum at halftime. Don't worry about it."

"Can we afford a maid and health insurance?"

"No point in putting the tools up until we finish the job. Tell
the kids to stay away from the band saw.
That could be dangerous."

"I was going to clean up the kitchen for you, but then I got
a call soliciting groceries for the food bank downtown, so I
raided the pantry. Do you have time to
drop these bags off for me?"

continued

"I'd like to help you wash those windows, but you
know how I feel about heights."

"I don't know how to fold sheets. It looks hard."

"I have no idea how to turn on that fancy washing
machine I bought you for Christmas."

"The cat keeps climbing in the litter box when I try to clean
it. I better let you handle that. The cat
likes you better anyway."

Housekeeping

Some love a good hotel for the location, view, or history. Others adore hotels for their restaurants, tennis courts, or swimming pools. My love of a hotel is encapsulated in just one word: *housekeeping*.

In fact, *housekeeping* may be my favorite word in the English language. Few things satisfy me more than chucking a wet towel onto the floor and knowing that a fluffy, fresh replacement will be hanging on the rod when I return; or lounging about in a huge bed with lots of pillows and then not making it up when I saunter out for the day. Better still, I adore eating a giant meal and not giving a second thought to the dishes. Replace the soap, clean the toilet, vacuum, mop, or dust? I'd prefer not to worry myself with such trivial matters.

Oh, don't look at me that way. You know you've done it: stolen hotel soap; used a white hand towel to remove your makeup; spilled some room-service ketchup on the floor and thought, "Eh, they'll get it." Hotels bring out our inner slobs.

Every now and then, I'll hang a hotel towel to reuse later, straighten the bedcovers, or maybe even consolidate all the trash into one can. "What consideration! What an environmentally sound guest!" I'll imagine the maids thinking as they clean the room.

The truth is, the maids think we're all pigs. Rock stars or librarians, CEOs or conventioneers, newlyweds or large families, we're all just messy human beings, leaving a trail of detritus as we amble through life. And seeing our mess—that awful slap of reality—takes us all down a notch in the maids' eyes. That's what Madame Cornuel meant when she said, "No man is a hero to his valet."

A woman said that, of course.

We men make messes. Big ones. Messes on a grand scale are part of our male nature. Fights, wars, wrecks, big emotional hullabaloos, and dirty socks left under the bed: that's us men. We gross ourselves out, which is why we expect your praise when we empty the dishwasher, scrub grout, or throw some Lysol in the toilet. Such actions go against our nature and seem monumental and heroic to us.

When we do monumental and heroic things, we men need praise: medals, ribbons, checks, bonuses, celebratory dinners, and access to a timeshare on the panhandle. Would a little congratulation when we Pledge the dining room table be so hard?

That need for recognition is a sure way to get a guffaw out of a group of women. "Jim scrubs the sink and thinks he deserves the National Medal of Honor." (Ensue hysterical laughter.)

There is no male counterpart to this phenomenon. I've never heard a man say, "Mary changed the oil in the Dodge and wants a gift certificate to the spa! Wha-ha-ha!"

Why is that?

Because most Marys don't change the oil in the Dodge or sharpen the mower blades. Most Susans don't edge along the driveway with a weed whacker. Most Jennifers wouldn't dream of cleaning the gutters or rewiring the light on the back stoop.

If our Marys, Jennifers, and Susans did those things, they could push most husbands over with a feather duster. And if a husband were to joke to his buddies about having to heap praise on his spouse for resetting the sprinkler system or replacing a rotten floor joist—he'd be met with stunned silence. "Sally knows how to miter a floor joist? That's so sexy!"

We don't get credit for our manly projects. They don't count. They're not considered "housekeeping." Never mind that many of them keep the actual house from collapsing, rotting into a heap of mold, or burning down in an electrical fire. Our Y-chromosome projects are called "fun," "gratifying," or worst of all (at least in feminine eyes), "puttering."

A woman scrubbing the sink = work.

A man fertilizing the lawn = puttering.

However unfair this characterization might seem, gentlemen, it is futile to try to recast the debate. We have lost the housekeeping argument. The modern man is expected to know his way around, and feel equally at ease with, a compressed-air-powered random orbital sander and a floating, cyclone-driven, swivel-head vacuum cleaner.

When faced with this defeat on the household front, I did the only thing a man in my position could do: I put out a want ad for a maid. Friends gave me unsolicited advice: "Forget it! You'll never get a good maid from the paper." Or, "Just hire a service." Or, "Nobody wants to work anymore. You won't get any takers." The most frequent complaint: "They won't clean."

Undeterred, I launched my carefully written, seventeen-word classified in *The Birmingham News*. "Wanted: Honest, sober person to clean tiny house for nice, neat couple. $10 per hour. Uniform provided."

Soon thereafter, I had a long list of candidates. My first hire was a large woman who identified herself as "Wunnaful Cook" on the phone. Hiring Wunnaful was a no-brainer to me, as she said bacon was her favorite food (mine, too). Unfortunately, Mrs. Murphy fired Wunnaful for showing up three weeks late to her first day on the job. So we moved on down the list to a woman named Betty. Betty lasted two days before getting sacked by Mrs. M. for trying to vacuum the dog. Then came Twanda. What a cleaner! She had our house spotless in no time. The place sparkled. So did Twanda herself—what a gorgeous woman. She shortened the hemline on her uniform by about three inches and was the talk of every husband in the neighborhood. I'm not quite sure what led to her demise, but I took it in stride and soldiered on down the list.

Mrs. Murphy kept dismissing maids for minor infractions such as not cleaning, not showing up, and stealing the silverware. For my part, I kept blithely buying uniforms (we have one in every size) and taking out classified ads.

Total disaster? Waste of money? Waste of time? Not at all. You see, it didn't matter if the "maid" knew the working end of a broom. It didn't matter if she took to drink and didn't show up for days on end. It didn't matter if she watched *Days of Our Lives* the entire time she was in our home. In short: I didn't care.

You see, by hiring a maid, I became something better than just a good helper around the house. I had become a super-husband. Yes, that's right. Men, just attempting to hire a domestic employee, regardless of the end result, is a major aphrodisiac for wives. I suddenly became the Brad Pitt of our supper club. Women pointed at me on the street. Ladies cooed and fluttered about like I was made of chocolate. If I added a line such as, "You know, Mrs. Murphy just works too hard to worry with housekeeping," or, "I don't want my wife ruining her expensive manicure scrubbing a toilet," I swear, I thought some of them were going to rip my clothes off on the spot.

Then, something entirely unexpected happened. We found a great maid. I mean a really fantastic person with a fabulous work ethic and a dynamic personality. Her name is Magaly. She is from Peru. We really adore her, and I cannot express how life changes for the better when someone else folds your socks. (I detest folding socks.) Every day, I tell Mrs. Murphy, "Don't fire Magaly," which has become a joke between us.

Unfortunately, I forgot to tell Mrs. Murphy a very important rule about maids, which almost destroyed my entire scheme. One night, at a dinner party, a guest asked my wife, "Do you have a good housekeeper?"

I could see Mrs. Murphy about to swoon over Magaly's talents. Panicked, I about flattened the centerpiece as I leaned over the table and blurted, "Yeah, our maid is okay, and pretty reliable when she's not drunk or in prison."

Mrs. Murphy looked at me, speechless. With my tie in the asparagus, I continued to bellow, "She's only broken a few things. Dear, wasn't it your grandmother's lamp that she knocked over? Or was it your favorite crystal vase?"

You see, Mrs. Murphy didn't know the cardinal rule of household help in Southern society: you never have a competent maid. There's always someone out there with more money and less scruples who will swipe your housekeeper faster than you can say *Bon Ami*.

So, through a careful campaign of deliberate bad-mouthing and general deceit, we've managed to keep our maid, which is a blessing beyond compare. One day I hope to have hot- and cold-running help—that, or retire to a hotel.

Until that day, as my Great Aunt Peggy says, our house is "clean enough to be sanitary and messy enough to be fun."

Secrets Men Know about Housekeeping

Dirty clothes, thrown on the floor, do walk to
the washer and dryer.

Shower mold, if left to its own devices, magically
disappears after a few weeks.

Breaking a few dishes is the surest way to
avoid dishwasher duty.

Nobody will know that you didn't wash the sheets if
you make the bed up *really nice*.

The Vacuum Fairy does exist and she does a great job.

Chapter 3

Getting Around

I Can't Get There
from Here

As much as I hate to confess it, I am, in fact, a living, breathing cliché: a woman with no sense of direction. I am one of those women who inspires chauvinistic, snickering men to blame women drivers for everything. I just read a newspaper article that claimed Saudi Arabian men blame Saudi Arabian women for most car accidents. That's right. Women can't legally DRIVE in Saudi Arabia, but the men feel that their spouses' backseat driving causes most of the accidents. This did not surprise me at all.

My husband, who has a wonderful sense of direction, naturally, finds it hard to believe that when I come to the end of the road, where I have to turn either left or right, and I have a fifty percent chance of getting it right, I somehow manage to get it wrong one hundred percent of the time. I tell him that it is like gambling against the house in Vegas. No matter what the odds are, the house always wins.

Almost no day goes by when I don't get lost somewhere in the errand running of my regular life. It's stressful. I envy those salmon and loggerhead turtles. They may not have opposable thumbs, but they are way ahead of me on the evolutionary tree. They can find their way home from anywhere on earth. I'd give anything to be able to do that.

Note: there are worse faults than having no sense of direction. I could be an embezzler of pension funds or a purse snatcher or just an all-around jerk. As fatal flaws go, I think I got off pretty light. So, although I occasionally have no idea where I am, it's really not that big of a deal in the grand scheme of things. I eventually end up somewhere vaguely familiar (you can't cross the border into another country without spotting some signs), or I ask someone for directions. I'll flag down a child on a bicycle if I have to. Almost anyone else has a better shot at getting it right than I do.

I've studied maps, twirled a few globes, and spent quality time trying to decipher the bus routes in the city where I live. The world is, apparently, filled with people who navigate with ease. School children do it. Half-crazy street people do it. Foreign visitors who can't read our English road signs speed fearlessly down the interstates. Young people, stupid people, old people, people with drug addictions, mentally ill people, physically handicapped people—it seems like all God's children EXCEPT me can navigate their way through life without too much trouble. If this was meant to be a humility lesson from the Almighty, I learned that lesson already. I wish we could move on to some of my other faults. It's not like I don't have a number of issues that require attention.

I could never have qualified as a pilot. There is no question I would have strayed accidentally into the airspace of a foreign nation and triggered an international incident. I could never have helped settle the West. I'd have been chucked out the back of a prairie schooner. From what I've read, there were precious few people to ask for directions. I would have stumbled into Indian Territory with nary a thought of a scalping, convinced we could all be friends. As a Southern woman, I could have shown those Indians a thing or two about sweet potatoes and brown sugar that would have bonded us for life.

It goes without saying that I could never drive a taxi. I'm not going to grow up to be a ballerina or an Olympic skier either. Those ships have sailed. We can't all do everything; can we? Unfortunately, the sad truth is that every job, even the ones I have as a mother and writer, requires *some* navigational skills, and I don't have any. It's upsetting.

Worst of all, I don't seem to be able to acquire the skills. I have always believed that I can learn anything from a book. I taught myself to repair sheetrock, to embroider pillowcases, and to write an Elizabethan sonnet (not a very good sonnet, but that is not really the point here) by reading. Astonishingly enough, I can learn how to make a nuclear bomb online, in case I have a pressing need for one of those. Navigation seems to be the one exception to the rule. Believe me when I tell you that you can't learn this from a book. You're either born with it, or you're not. I missed out on some chromosomal material, and I feel a little bit cheated.

All I can do now is to try and compensate for my birth defect the same way that other heroines throughout history have worked to overcome theirs. This I do as only a control-freak Southern woman can do. I have stacks of index cards with directions filed away. I can Google my way out of a paper bag. If I had to load up a backpack with emergency supplies, the first thing I'd pack is my GPS device. Add an emergency supply of chocolate, and I'd be good to go.

GPS technology changed my life. Sure, satellites have been good for mass-communication companies, cruise missiles, and fishing boats, but I don't think we can overlook the life-changing applications of modern technology for suburban women like me. I carry a GPS unit in my purse at all times as if I am a soldier in Afghanistan trying to avoid an ambush by hostile bands of wandering militia. If I could convince a veterinarian to implant one of those GPS trackers under my skin the way they do for pets, I'd jump up on the exam table in a heartbeat. I'd love to call up the vet's office, tell them I'm lost, and have them send someone to pick me up.

With my GPS, I climb in the car with no worries. All I need is a street address. In a pinch, I can go with just a zip code. Heck, if I'm going somewhere famous, I don't need anything but a name. I crank up the car, plug in my GPS, wait for the green-to-go satellite triangulation, and head out without even planning which way to back out of the driveway.

Once you get over the no-sense-of-direction stress, driving can be fun. It's like getting on a ride at Disney World. It's always a little adventure. The screen shows a reassuring picture of my car toodling along a highlighted route at all times.

Best of all, my GPS talks to me. It's better than the crooning words of a lover. We share a deep, meaningful relationship. It never yells at me. If I somehow manage to stray from its painstaking directions, it stays with me. That's the beauty of the system. It isn't married, like some men I know, to the pre-planned route. It doesn't care where we are going or what time we will arrive. It cares only about what I am doing at all times. Me, me, me. Lovely.

The worst thing it says, when it is totally flummoxed by my inability to follow the simplest of directions is, "Please make a U-turn as soon as safely possible." That is polite GPS-speak for, "Nobody in the world has managed to screw this up worse than you. I've helped loads of people. Some of them couldn't speak English. One woman was driving herself home from her own cataract surgery. I knew on the first day when you could not even get me out of the box that this was going to be the worst assignment ever. I have a cousin guiding cruise missiles and a brother working for NASA. Working with you is a waste of raw talent."

I've learned to ride with others whenever possible, and I've been told on more than one occasion that I am a charming passenger. You'll never hear me criticize another driver's navigational choices. I just admire the scenery.

Those of you lucky enough to be born with instinctive compasses encoded in the wrinkles of your brains don't have a clue about the trials those of us without any homing instincts go through. I could not make the grade as a pigeon. Think about that sentence for a minute. You don't get much lower on the food chain than a pigeon.

I wouldn't wish this problem on my worst enemy. Most

people seem to think it is perfectly fine to yell at directionally challenged people. It's pretty insensitive when you think about it and not at all in tune with a twenty-first-century sense of social enlightenment. Think about it. How would you feel about someone yelling at a paraplegic: "Hey, why don't you get out of that wheelchair and walk, you big faker?" None of you would think that kind of talk is civilized; would you? Is my handicap so different?

One of my closest friends (let's call her Laura since that is her real name, and she deserves to be outed for her intolerant behavior) doesn't even pretend to be nice to me when I call her for help in a navigational emergency. She starts yelling immediately.

"Where are you right now?" she demands. "How could you possibly have screwed this up? A kindergartener could do this. You do not have walking-around sense. I am amazed every day that you do not get run over by a truck. Am I going to have to get in my car and come get you? I just put on my sweatpants. I'll talk you through it one stop sign at a time. You are not safe to be let out on your own," she says.

It's a good thing that one of my sins isn't pride. You can't have too much pride if you have a poor sense of direction.

People who have a good sense of direction can't seem to comprehend that everyone else doesn't share their God-given abilities. "What is wrong with you? Are you stupid? How could you not know how to drive home from here?" they ask, askance.

"I have no sense of direction," I reply in a calm voice, trying to rise above their juvenile taunts to explain the problem in a dignified manner. "It's a handicap I was born with, like bushy eyebrows or eleven toes." I always add in a morally superior tone, hoping to make my tormentor feel at least a twinge of guilt, "It's not nice to make fun of handicapped people."

If you have a navigational handicap like I do, you dread having to drive, fly, or walk anywhere new, especially if there is a timeline involved that doesn't allow for any "lost" time, no matter how early you set out (the cruise ship will leave the dock, for example). When I signed the contract agreeing to the terms for the sale of my first book, I wasn't nervous about writing deadlines, television or radio interviews, or public speaking engagements. I was worried about finding the venues I would have to locate in cities and states where I would be promoting my book.

You better believe that I didn't sign that contract until I had a volunteer driver lined up. I knew I would end up getting lost. I was right, too. I've been lost in cities all over the South. I'd like to take a moment right here to thank each and every one of you who helped me find somewhere I had to be along the way. Like Blanche du Bois in *A Streetcar Named Desire*, I, too, have always depended upon the kindness of strangers. Well, not *exactly* like her. You know what I mean. I'd hop in a car with Attila the Hun if he promised to drive me over the Alps to a village book signing. And don't think I haven't contemplated picking up a hitchhiker for navigational help. I haven't actually pulled over, but I've thought about it. It's not something I'm particularly proud of.

It's hard to live with a fatal flaw. Society is intolerant, impatient, and downright snippy. Directionally challenged women like me need a few minutes when the light changes from red to green to decide where to go next. For us, every turn is a fifty-fifty shot in the dark. Next time you are tempted to honk, have a heart. We may be contemplating bigger things than whether to turn or go straight. Some of us are trying to remember what city we're in. Once a year, just because you can when so many of us can't, say, "Follow me!" to some lost soul, and lead her back to civilization.

Lost

Lost. Who, me? Never. I always know where I am, especially if I'm behind the wheel of an automobile. I don't need your expensive GPS device. I don't like disembodied voices saying things such as, "Bear right in two hundred yards," as if while hurdling along at seventy miles per hour, I could visually paint imaginary stripes on the roadway, yard by yard. Please. The GPS voice might as well say, "First down!" when I fly past the exit. Nor does my rearview mirror house a digital compass—what good does it do me to know that the Stop-and-Stab gas station sits in a southeasterly direction?

Sure, I possess an uncanny talent for map reading, probably left over from my days as a Boy Scout when I wandered the piney woods of South Alabama with nothing but a battered scrap of map and a tin compass. Yet, I don't *need* maps.

The navigational truth: I'm a Southern male. I go places in a manner that suggests I know where I'm headed. I don't sneak into rooms or meekly slide into church pews. I don't shy around corners or slouch down corridors. I bust open doors, stride down halls, stomp across parking lots, bluster through supermarket aisles, and purposefully make my way through crowds. No dithering, no wavering, no listing about, no aimless wandering, and most of all, no stopping and asking for directions.

I know, I know, many of you are rolling your eyes to heaven (it won't get you there any faster, as Mama says). Why won't men stop and ask for directions? What harm could there be in that?

I'll tell you the harm, lady. Asking for directions implies that you *have* no direction. "Oh, that's silly," I can hear you muttering from here. No, madam, it isn't. A man's man doesn't go about life directionless. A man's man has purpose. He knows where he's going. He gets there. He isn't lost.

Lost. It's a four-letter word to men. "He's lost," remains the very worst thing one man can say about another. Let me translate this for you: a Southern man saying, "He's lost" is the equivalent of a Southern woman saying, "She's tacky."

You can't recover from "lost."

So no, I don't like stopping and asking for directions. Besides, I don't get lost. I may be temporarily waylaid, somewhat off course, slightly detained, in uncharted waters, vaguely unsure of the fastest route to my ultimate destination, or beyond cell-phone range, but I am emphatically, definitely, never lost.

Before I give you an example of not being lost, let me preface it with some background. I once dabbled as an automotive journalist, mainly for the perk of driving free cars. Yes, automotive journalists receive test cars to borrow and drive about randomly. Nice cars. This gravy train with biscuit wheels came in handy to me, the penniless writer. It gave me the appearance of being a man of means, which is the primal reason that men drive fancy cars. Well, actually, the girls admire the fancy car, and that's probably the primal reason. Other guys admire the wheels, too. The doorman at Mrs. Murphy's building presumed that I, a broke writer, was, in fact, the richest guy in Manhattan. Why? Because every week I arrived in a new car. "Hey! Mr. Murphy, what did you do with the Porsche Carrera?" he'd ask as I pulled up in a Cadillac DeVille. "Oh, the ashtrays were full," I'd casually respond. The next week he'd say, "Hey,

Mr. Murphy! What did you do with the Caddy?" as I lumbered up the drive in a Mercedes SL500. "Eh, the color was a tad too drab for me." This went on for years.

So back to our narrative: While on my honeymoon in France, the good people of Bentley offered to lend me a giant, hulking piece of British motordom. That's right—they offered to loan me a car that cost more than a nice-sized house. Naturally, I said *oui*. Who wouldn't want to play the part of an eccentric English *bon vivant* tooling about Froggyland in a beast of a British car?

Mrs. Murphy, as it turns out.

She was terrified that we'd run over some Frenchie cyclist or wind up with a Renault stuck in our radiator grill. And though both scenarios were real possibilities in Paris, the further we drove from the City of Lights, the more relaxed Mrs. Murphy became. Soon, she stopped fretting and settled into the soft hides of the monster Bentley. I hummed along to French radio, and presently we were making great time toward our destination, Mont-Saint-Michel, a picturesque island on the French coast. (*Making great time*, by the way, ranks in order of importance to men slightly above changing the oil regularly and a whisper below obedience to the Almighty.) Gradually, French interstates became highways. Highways became roadways. Roadways became, well, slightly overgrown paths. That's when the low-petrol light winked on.

Undeterred, I joked that the Bentley probably had a good ten or twenty gallons left, given that the enormous car only attained eight miles to the imperial gallon. (There's another lesson here about how young men like to find out how far they can go on one tank of gas. Older men, perhaps as a result of long-smoldering fights, always fill up at half-a-tank). In any event, this news did not have a calming effect on my new bride. She immediately began clamoring that I should find a gas station. Unfortunately, lest the Lord bestowed a French cow with the divine gift of petroleum udders, there was no go-juice to be found. We had no choice but to ooze on in the Bentley.

Moments later, Mrs. Murphy began a campaign for me to

stop and ask for directions to the nearest gas station. I politely demurred. She persisted. I refused. She insisted. I resisted. She told me, "Morgan Murphy, stop this car right this instant and find out where we are!" I stopped. I put the Bentley in park. You could hear the clock ticking in the walnut-veneered dash. I turned to face my beautiful new bride.

"We are in France," I said . . . and quickly surmised from her expression that if I were to remain married more than the five days we'd made it thus far as a couple, I needed to add a little something more to that statement. I continued, ". . . in the gorgeous countryside, ensconced in a car that costs more than a house, with a trunk full of cheese and wine. We have no place to go, nowhere to be. What could be better than to run out of gas right here, with you?"

That did the trick.

But forget all that lovey-dovey garbage: we weren't lost. The road only went in two directions—forward and backward. We'd traveled the backward bit—no gas stations there. So it was forward or farmland—no other choice to be made. And besides, my French is *tres mal*. I can barely ask for a cheese sandwich, much less understand words such as, "Go left at the first farm; then hang a right in the town of Sheep's Gout."

The romantic gesture bought me a little time to get back on course. Happily for me, a gas station soon appeared. A few minutes and one hundred francs later, we were on Mont St. Michelle eating giant, fluffy omelets at La Mere Poulard, watching the tide wash out.

Had we been lost? I'll never tell.

What to Say When She Says, "We're Lost"

"But dear, we can't be lost. We're Presbyterian."

"Not really. I see the sun is approximately forty-three
degrees over the horizon, meaning we're
headed in the right direction."

"Nah, we're just temporarily unfamiliar with
our surroundings."

"That's what the highway department wants us to believe."

" 'Lost' is a matter of opinion."

Chapter 4

On the Prowl

A Shopping Philosophy

The primary difference between the way men and women shop lies in an underlying assumption. Men shop with an end result in mind. They head to the mall like Neanderthal man ran from the cave—at a dead run, armed with a club, eyes on the prize. Regardless of what they are shopping for, most men think of shopping as a duty, and they plan each trip like a military mission. Their goal is to canvass the sale ads in the newspaper, locate the item they need at the lowest price, secure a good parking spot near the store, and identify the shortest route in and out of the building like scouts darting behind enemy lines. Men scope out the shortest, cash-only checkout line so they can be home before halftime is over.

When they return to their man caves, men will have exactly what they left to buy—no more, no less. Unless tempted by shiny new toys—a fancy new barbeque grill, for example—most men are not impulse buyers. They do not want to debate the advantages of grills with a flat black paint finish versus grills with a glossy black paint finish. As far as I can tell, men do not have strong feelings about the colors of their grills or household appliances.

Generally speaking, men do not like to browse. Women do. This is a big distinction. Men have no desire to indulge in time-wasting chitchat with sales clerks or fellow shoppers. Shopping is not a social activity for men. They see the necessity of it. They want new stuff. They see shopping as a legal way to acquire material possessions—as opposed to clubbing someone over the head for them—but it is merely a necessary evil that must be endured to provide goods for their families. Many men simply cannot conceive of shopping for fun.

With all the predatory instincts men have, you'd think they'd enjoy shopping more. Shopping is the ultimate treasure hunt. Retailers conspire against us with product placement, misleading advertising, and colorful lures to get us into their stores. We consumers have to use all our wiles and intellect to triumph over temptation. Doesn't that seem like a game men would dearly love? I know women who love the thrill of the hunt. The mere rumor of half-price footwear has caused women I know to sneak out of Sunday-morning church services (hunched over in a vain attempt to remain unnoticed, creeping to the back of the church on their tiptoes, car keys and credit cards clutched tightly in their hot little hands) before the final amen has finished ricocheting off the walls. For skillful shoppers, there is just no fun in paying full price for anything. Any idiot with a checkbook can do that. Champagne taste and a beer budget—there's the challenge.

There are some exceptions to my shopping generalizations, of course. Most men will happily spend hours shopping for fishing, hunting, or golf paraphernalia. They also like to check out new cars and boats. They're willing to spend hours in stores that offer rubber waders, fishing lures, and graphite drivers. In these stores, men turn into the most social of animals. They're eager to trade stories with the salesmen about horsepower, antlers, the fish that got away, and the hole in one that no one saw. I'm not even going to try to psychoanalyze this behavior. In my opinion, men could not be any more obvious if they tried.

It is true that women mission shop, too, upon occasion.

Every woman I know has woken up on at least one morning of her life and discovered with horror that the dress she planned to wear to a party that night can no longer be zipped up due to overindulgence in all things delicious. This is perfectly understandable. It can happen to anyone. Let me tell you that you do not want to get in the way of a chubby woman who has nothing to wear to a party, a woman with two measly hours to shop before she has to pick up her children from school. She doesn't have time to dither. She needs a dressing room, an assortment of sizes, a coupon for at least twenty percent off, and room to move.

Some mission-shopping assignments are harder than others. Every December, when small children start making lists for Santa, parents everywhere know they are about to be tested. My daughter once asked Santa to bring her hot-pink winter gloves with green fingers. When I hinted that Santa might not have in stock exactly what my daughter had in mind, she looked at me like she felt sorry for me, a grown-up with so little faith in Santa. "Of course, Santa will bring them, Mommy. That's what Santa *does*," she reminded me. Well, duh.

Another year my middle child refused to tell anyone except Santa, the fat man himself, what he wanted for Christmas. Think about that for a minute. This presented some logistical problems, which resulted in my tampering with the United States mail one dark, cold night. I was nervous about committing a federal offense, and I was grateful not to be caught in the act. My middle child is just the type to press charges. He's a stickler for privacy. As Santa's Little Helper, I ask you: what choice did I have?

Generally, for women, it's not the purchase of one specific item that makes a shopping trip successful. I once sallied forth to buy running sneakers and came home with a set of matching, hand-painted chopsticks for the entire family. The chopsticks were half price and exquisite. I wish I could show them to you. You would see instantly that I made the right choice, even if my husband could not appreciate it at the time. Every woman I know will understand how such a thing could happen. A shopping list is merely a guide, you know. It's not holy writ.

Women have learned to take advantage of what's available, on sale, fresh, easy to carry, unlikely to spoil, and a big enough size for both kids to wear. In some countries, women get in line with a shopping basket without even knowing what they are standing in line for. Whatever it is, they are bound to need it.

Most women (and some men, even straight men) shop for entertainment. I do. My favorite place to shop is Scott's Antique Market in Atlanta, Georgia. I like to make a day of it. For me, shopping there is like eye candy for my brain and soul. It's relaxing, a great stress reliever. My mind is fed such a colorful, thought-provoking stream of stimuli that there is no room in my head to worry about real-life problems. It's a treat to live totally in the moment for a few hours. Who doesn't love a little escapism? There are dealers at Scott's from all over the world. You never know what you will see, things you can afford and things that are wildly expensive. I've seen an authentic suit of armor, a stuffed leopard, a poison ring, and piles of jewelry that look like something out of the Pirates of the Caribbean ride at Disney World. Even if I don't buy a thing, I have fun. Part of the fun for me is that there are European-style bakeries on site. Eating and shopping together are one of life's most pleasurable combinations. (Now that I think about it, I may be sorry I told you about Scott's. It's crowded enough already.)

Like almost every woman I know, I love to shop. Chalk up another cliché with my name on it. Add it to the pile—chocolate, bubble bath, and sappy movies. I'm not ashamed. I want to go inside every bookstore I walk by, plop down my credit card, and buy a stack of books. I'd rather shop for shoes than anything else on earth, and I like shopping for antiques so much I even watch *Antiques Roadshow* on television if I stumble across it with the remote control. (I have no idea when anything actually airs on television. Do you? I guess that is why God made TiVo, one of the greatest inventions ever.)

So what? As a self-appointed spokeswoman for my fellow

shoppers, I'd like to suggest that maybe we are more than just living, breathing, shopping clichés. Maybe we women are just right about shopping and a lot of other things. Did you ever think of that?

A List of Hard-to-Find Items

Body-shaper or control-panel lingerie. If you've ever needed these undergarments, you know why they're on the list. If you've never even heard of them, don't ask questions. You do not want to know.

Ice bags that conform to sore muscles without leaking and heating pads that don't (a) set the house on fire when exposed to vast clouds of hair spray or (b) singe the fur of the cat caught napping on the "high heat" setting.

Buttons. Throughout history, cheap buttons have ruined more expensive outfits than costume jewelry.

Men. I know a woman who shopped online for a man with nice table manners, a steady job, and his own hair. Sure, she heard from a few freaks, but, eventually, she found an accountant she adores. He was a good buy.

Gutter rakes. My husband insisted there was no such thing, but I knew that I was not the only woman to balk at cleaning gutters. A quick Internet search revealed: gutter rakes, $9.99, plus shipping and handling. We could save a lot of time if my husband listened to me better.

Flu vaccines. If you get a tip that nurses are at the grocery store jabbing customers in the produce aisle, head over there like somebody has just spotted Elvis.

Artificial Christmas trees that look "just like the real thing." A fake tree looks fake. If you don't want the expense and mess of a live tree, get over it. You cannot have it all.

The perfect present to make up for forgetting your anniversary. This is like Bigfoot. It doesn't exist. Apologize profusely, and mark your calendar with a big horse's behind to remind yourself next year.

You Need a Retail Therapist

Morgan Murphy

Why do men hate to shop? Dr. Murphy has the answer.

They are scarred, early in life, by shopping experiences with their mothers. They are dragged to smelly fabric stores where they get in trouble for building a fort out of bolts of burlap. Young boys rebel when placed into a shopping-buggy seat, a piece of plastic sticky from the diapers and germs of zillions of other whining children, their chubby legs uncomfortably poking through the chilly frames of the steel carts. They are traumatized by a stroll through the Sears lingerie department.

Then, suddenly, as a teenager, young men are liberated from shopping. Ah, freedom. No need to go to the grocery store (Mom does it). No need to go clothes shopping (Mom does it). No need to go to the lingerie department (Victoria's Secret sends it to Mom). But girls go to the mall; in fact, they roam the mall in hoards. So boys find themselves, once again, headed to the mall out of sheer desperation to catch a woman's attention between sales.

The mall: for me, the mall must be the seventh layer of hell. Mr. and Mrs. Big Butt America amble through the mall pointing at glow-in-the-dark garden frogs and admiring giant beanbags imprinted with the names and mascots of their favorite college football teams. They walk slowly, Mr. and Mrs. Big Butt. They block traffic. They don't stick to the right lane, keeping harried writers from dashing for the exit into the light of the world.

If pressed, I'll admit that there are some redeeming parts of the mall. The food court may rank as one. I love a good food court, despite its ridiculous name, as if McDonald's is royalty. "Sir Hamburgler, prithy would you tell Lady Taco that we'd like to have a word with her by the largest indoor merry-go-round?"

And then there's the Apple Store. Men like computer stores. Those are usually in malls. Restoration Hardware—that's not much of a hardware store anymore—but you can still find men gathered there in a mall, like survivors of atomic warfare huddled in a nuclear fallout shelter. Restoration Hardware should come up with a "manly corner" where a man can hide with other men until his wife emerges from the French Connection.

In all honesty, however, it is a fallacy that men don't like to browse. Some New Age expert invented that bunk. Men love to shop and to browse. Need proof? Visit your average Lowe's or Home Depot. A man will say, "I'm going out to get some quarter-round molding for the porch," and come back three days later with a new garden hose, a zero-radius-riding John Deere, a pack of one-hundred-watt lightbulbs (long may they shine), six hundred solid-brass wood screws, and a new cooler. Of course, he will have forgotten the quarter-round molding.

Or head to a car lot. Yes, that's shopping. Men don't want to admit looking for a new car is shopping—but it is. Women, if you want to get a guilt-free pass on all the shoes you purchase for the next four years, be supportive when the man in your life wants to buy a car with all the buttons. We love buttons. Buttons to us are like Jimmy Choos to women. You can never have enough buttons on your automobile.

Lastly, a saunter through the Bass Pro Shop will reveal the inner shopping diva in most men. Big burly men get positively giddy and skip around like thirteen-year-old girls in the Bass Pro Shop. The Cold War was fought with less stuff than they have in there.

I'm sorry to admit it, but what men really hate to do is shop for you. Shopping for a woman is a nerve-racking and ego-busting experience. Firstly, it requires us to go to shops that we don't like to be seen in (see above). Secondly, women are pickier than men when it comes to gifts.

The typical man doesn't return anything, ever. That's why when I walk into a Macy's, the shopkeepers flock to me like I'm made of $100 bills. They know that if a man buys something, he'll never bring it back. Make a sale and it's good in perpetuity. The shopkeepers also know that a man is uncomfortable in Macy's and will purchase nearly anything so he can get the hell out of there. This makes for a *fast* sale. Another plus. Smart salespeople spend their days tackling men who come into the store.

Women are a lousy bet if you're a salesperson. They linger and browse, debate and mull. When they do finally buy something, they very well may be back the next day to return it (after all, it's another chance to go to the store). I believe this phenomenon is why department stores make it so absolutely miserable to return items, with the paperwork, the manager's signature, the original credit card you purchased the item with, your address, your telephone number.

We men know this about women, of course. We learned it early, at our mothers' sides. So when it comes to buying you a gift, we know that there's a very strong possibility that you will want to return it. It's very unsettling, that. As a young newlywed, it took me years to figure out what Mrs. Murphy might like for birthdays, anniversaries, etc. I finally wised up and bought her stuff that she'd registered for at the time of our wedding but never received. That way, *she'd picked it out*. Clever, eh? Some women complain that the men in their lives buy them the same thing every year for their birthday, Christmas, etc. This is normal. If you fawn over our initial gift of perfume, scarf, small handbag, we men will buy you that item for the rest of eternity. Mrs. Murphy admired those Christmas-time Byer figures from *A Christmas Carol*. So one year I bought her Tiny Tim and his dad, Bob Cratchet, which elicited squeals of excitement on Christmas morning and a big hug. The next year, I bought her Scrooge. Then Marley the next. Then the Fezywhigs. After a few more years, we were into the ghosts. Christmas Past was a pretty lady in a white dress. Christmas Present was a fat dude carrying lots of food. But I had a problem with Christmas Future. I just couldn't imagine giving my wife the Grim Reaper for Christmas: "Merry Christmas, honey, I bought you DEATH." But I was torn, because the Ghost of Christmas Future is an integral part of the story (and I am a storyteller, after all).

So I put a bottle of her favorite perfume in there with Mr. Sickle, and that seemed to take the edge off, so to speak.

But I'm nearly out of characters. I'm down to the minor leagues. Last year, I bought the little boy who buys the Christmas goose. We're running out of room on the table, in fact, and our house runs the risk of looking like a Victorian bed-and-breakfast. So it appears I'll be forced to do something ambitious, bold, and somewhat scary: go shopping.

Chapter 5

What the #*$&?

Watch Your Mouth

I have no desire whatsoever to write this chapter. I am writing it under duress. My coauthor picked this topic. Since I chose almost all the other topics in this book, it seemed nice to throw him a bone. Morgan is convinced we should tackle this subject. He really thinks writing about profanity is a good idea.

He's wrong, of course.

I am surprised that he didn't instantly give in on this one. He's been well trained by at least three generations of bossy, Southern matrons to do what the women in his life want him to do. Most of the time, he does what I want him to do. It saves time in the long run. It is easier, I think, just to give us what we want at the outset. Odds are, we Southern women will get what we want in the end, so why not just take a shortcut to the conclusion? It's more efficient.

This incident has given me pause. I'm a little bit worried. It is possible that my writing partner may be one of those men I can only push so far before he draws a line in the sand and dares me, politely, of course, to step across it with my expensively shod feet. Apparently, he's waiting patiently right across the line in his huge wing tips to take me on. Up until now, we've been sailing along, amused at one another's take on similar subjects, but not overly concerned about the other's views. In this chapter, however, we are poles (as in North and South) apart.

Even when I disagree with Morgan's viewpoints, I find him charming. He always disagrees with me nicely, as only a Southern man can. I love how he takes the blame for everything. A misunderstanding about the time we were to meet? He must have misheard. One of us needs to cut a few paragraphs? Obviously, it should be him. Somebody forgot to feed the parking meter? We all know who the culprit is.

I never said the man doesn't have nice manners. He has, in fact, *exquisite* manners. I hope my boys grow up to be just like him. It takes a lot of skill, cunning, tact, flattery, and cash to keep your grandmother, mother, wife, sister, and writing partner happy. I have been told on very good authority that I am a full-time job all by myself. This man has to keep his day job humming along and serve with the United States Navy one weekend a month to defend our country from enemies both foreign and domestic. Keeping me sweet is small potatoes, when you think about it.

I'm fretting over this chapter. First, I said, "No, thanks." Then, I said, "I don't believe I want to write about that, thank you." Finally, I said, "I'm not going to write about that, and you can't make me." I turned up my nose, rolled my eyes, and made "icky" noises with my throat. In the end, I told Morgan he would likely sprout wings and fly before I'd write this chapter.

That's when an astonishing thing happened. In a velvety, deep-bass drawl I adore, my friend looked across the desk at me and said, between his teeth, "Yes. We. Are. Writing. This. Chapter."

I thought I was going to have to take to my bed. I really did.

I was torn about how to respond. I couldn't decide if I wanted to throw a full-scale hissy fit or just give in to save face. The men in my life rarely say no to me. I'm not accustomed to it, frankly. It's going to take some getting used to. It seems that I have been overruled. Usually, it works like this: I try on two different shoes I am contemplating wearing and ask my husband which he likes better with the outfit. When he chooses one, I invariably know I want to wear the other. He never bats an eyelash; he always says, "Glad to be of service." In a way, I am like the United States Supreme Court. I am not used to reconsidering my own seasoned, well-reasoned, beautifully argued, and obviously correct conclusions to entertain the possibility that I might be misguided, uninformed, or just plain pigheaded or wrong.

In the end, I decided to take it on the chin. I am a professional writer. I can write about anything. Theoretically, I could write about a weekend of professional (oxymoron—emphasis on the *moron* part—coming up here) wrestling, couldn't I? And if I could write about wrestling or NASCAR or Hollywood movie stars or ridiculous fluff like that, surely I can handle a chapter on something as lowbrow as profanity; don't you agree?

Since I am being dragged into this chapter kicking and screaming, I'm just going to come right out and tell it like it is. I don't know how we've come to this. I really don't. As far as I can determine, the use of profanity has become so commonplace, so ordinary, and so run of the mill that it is now socially acceptable to swear anywhere, anytime, and in almost any circumstance. I'm appalled. One Sunday, during a special service at my church, a professional musician chimed in a little early with his instrument, and the whole congregation caught a whiff of a four-letter word. That's right. Swearing in the house of the Lord. Those microphones are more sensitive than you think. It doesn't get much lower than swearing in church. He should have just headed on up to the altar rail to pray about it. I thought about dragging him up there by his ear for a "come to Jesus" moment. He better be glad he wasn't riding home with me.

Most irritating of all, I think, is the fact that profanity is now used as a space-filler in ordinary conversation. If I'm going to swear, it has to mean something. I have to believe that nothing else will do but that particular swearword to make my point effectively. That's not true for everyone. You can tell. Most swearing is completely thoughtless. While it is true that a vast majority of Americans fill conversational pauses with a never-ending stream of *you know, I mean, anyway,* and my personal pet peeve, the albatross of the sixties, the ever-popular, meaningless, space-filling *like* and *man.* You might hear, for example, "Like, you know, man, I just said #$%@!! that, man! I'm not taking this @&*%!!" Impressive, isn't it? Makes you want to hire that person to represent your company or bring him or her home to meet your family; doesn't it?

The bar has been lowered every year. It must be flat on the ground by now. When I was a young woman in the South, you rarely heard men swear in public, and you never heard ladies swear. That's no longer true, which is not exactly what I was hoping for when I said I wanted the same opportunities as the men in my class. I can recall being in the student section at a University of Alabama football game when I heard a young fraternity boy swear out loud over a missed tackle. A few seconds later, I distinctly remember the profanity being followed by a loud, "Excuse me, ladies!" Thirty years later, my boys report hearing "Bull$@$%!" from the student section, routinely.

My children don't react to public expressions of profanity anymore, except maybe to check my emotional temperature to see if I am going to embarrass them in public with more of my outdated, old-fashioned expectations of public morality. (They know it takes every bit of self-control I possess not to pull up the pants of a teenage boy who is standing in front of me showing off his underwear. My kids know that if I actually know that boy, if he has slept under my roof or put his feet under my dinner table, then I'm going to *tell* him to pull his pants up.)

How did we come to this? Am I the only mother out there insisting that her teenagers swim against the cultural tide? I often feel that I am. "Are you that stupid?" I always ask my children when this subject comes up. "Do you have such a tiny vocabulary that you can't come up with your own adjectives? You have been expensively educated. Has it all been for nothing? Don't you have an original thought in your head? Are you so small brained that you can't come up with a single witty comeback?" I demand.

I recently spent time waiting for one of my children in the parking lot of his high school, and I counted the F-bomb being tossed carelessly out in public at least ten times—by boys and girls. I'll have you know that I was over forty years old before I used that word in the complete privacy of my very own closet. I was alone. I was really mad, and I still felt guilty about *thinking* it, much less *saying* it out loud.

Of course, banning profanity in my own home results in its own unique firestorm of teenage revenge. It goes without saying that if you ban profanity for the masses, you can't use it either, and you'll suffer, believe me, if you ever let anything slip in front of your kids. The most benign swearing will draw pious looks, shameful finger wagging, and demands for an increase in allowance to insure they don't "accidentally" reveal your linguistic slip to siblings.

When a ticked-off high school boy gets in my car after three hours of hot, sweaty football practice, I have to be ready to pounce on, "My coach is a —" with a gentle reminder. I raise my eyebrows into my hairline, lift a finger in warning, and threaten my child with a look that says, "Tread carefully, son." I've learned to live with on-the-fly rephrasing like, "My coach is a m-ean f-isted son of a b-east" and pretend like it makes perfect sense. It's the polite thing to do.

The Polite Way to Curse

Since I have taken a stand against profanity, it seems only fair that I supply the world with some good euphemisms. The following list is a tried-and-true compilation used by a bevy of Southern women I know and love. Remember that almost any word can be uttered as an effective swearword. It's all in the tone, vehemence, and decibel level you choose to deliver it. A lot of swearing is just theater. A little finger pointing goes a long way. Some of my favorite socially acceptable (or marginally acceptable, at the very worst) expressions are:

Dadgummit. This is a catchall expression in the South, used by men and women alike, to reveal anything from mild disgust to boiling rage, depending upon the provocation. For example, you might hear, "*Dadgummit,* I dropped my church bulletin," or "Now wait just a *dadgum* minute, missy!"

Dang it or *darn it*. These are sanitized versions of the D-word for citizens of all ages when nothing more creative comes to mind. Example: "Throw me the *dang* life vest before I drown!"

Goodnight nurse. No idea about the derivation of this one, but it's colorful. It is most often used when one's ire is mixed with humor. The speaker is totally exasperated. Example: "*Goodnight nurse*, man! You can't shoot the woman for talking too much. It's illegal."

Jesus, Mary, and Joseph. This is not meant to be sacrilegious at all. It is the expression you use when you need to call on the Son of God and both of his earthly parents to help you deal with some mess that has rocked you to your foundation, as in, "*Jesus, Mary, and Joseph*! I wish I'd knocked on that bedroom door before I opened it on those two naked men."

Mercy me. This phrase is used by women, primarily, or very effeminate men. It is actually a shorthand version of a prayer, as in "Have mercy on me, Lord." It's kind of a wimpy expression. Self-explanatory, I think. Example: "*Mercy me*, sister, do we dare open another bottle of wine?"

Land's sake! or, in the extreme version, *land's sake alive!* You almost never hear this expression anymore except out of the mouths of little old ladies. It's a shame. I miss it. I think it originates from immigrants spotting the shores of the New World for the first time, as in "Look there! Finally! We made it alive to dry land! We can stop throwing up now."

Oh, my goodness, or *for goodness sake*. Clearly, this has religious overtones. It's all about goodness and mercy in all the great religions, I've noticed. I guess that's why all of the best swearwords call on the Almighty to resolve things. Example: "*For goodness sake*, don't just stand there and look at it. Kill it before it bites you."

Oh, my, or *oh, my stars*. This is usually said by a Southern woman who is so flummoxed by a situation that she cannot think of one other word to say. Her hands are often plastered to her cheeks, and her mouth often gapes open in shock when she is forced to use this kind of language. Sometimes, she is just embarrassed, as in, "*Oh, my stars*, I cannot believe that pretty young girl used that word in front of God and everybody. I was married for twenty-seven years before I even knew what it meant!"

Lawsy, lawsy. This is a Southern consonant softening of *oh, Lordy, Lordy*. It is uttered most effectively while one shakes one's head from side to side, with one's eyes firmly fixed on one's feet. The translation is something along the lines of, "I do not know how you have come to the point of shoplifting. They are going to carry you off to prison for sure."

Well, I never. This is shorthand for, "I have never seen such a ridiculous thing in all my life. That is some kind of sex I have never heard of before. What were they thinking?"

I Swear

Warning: this chapter is rated PG for mild profanity.

I am a man, a Southerner, and a sailor in the United States Navy, so yes, I swear. Now before you turn the page with indignant outrage, allow me to elaborate on the art of Southern swearing. For there does exist a proper time and place for swearing. Furthermore, I know you've cussed, probably today. So I'm here to help because good cussing can be an art form, no matter how profane that might seem.

Melinda, as befits her gender and upbringing, rightly abhors indiscriminate profanity. No self-respecting Southern lady, no paragon of Southern femininity, enjoys what I call carpet-bomb cussing. You hear it on television, read it in magazines, see it mouthed by other drivers in traffic. We live in a torrent of brief Anglo-Saxon utterances, a river of vile profanity.

I'm not talking about thoughtless invective. I'm talking about useful, restorative, wholesome, and altogether-useful cussing. For example, I've heard my grandmother swear. One day, when I was about seven years old, she asked me to change a lightbulb that dangled from an old-fashioned cord in her junk room. I unscrewed the burned-out bulb, and as I was about to screw in its replacement, Grandmother said, "Morgan, stick your finger in the socket and see if it's on." Grandmama didn't have a death wish for me. She was and is simply one of those Southern ladies who doesn't know the working end of a screwdriver. Wisely, I suggested that perhaps I wasn't tall enough to reach the socket. Exasperated, Grandmother replied, "I'll do it then." She climbed the stepladder, inserted one gloved finger into the socket, and WHAM! About 120 volts hit her like a late-model Oldsmobile. As she was thrown from the ladder, she hollered, "Damnation!"

Years later, I consider her brief utterance a testament to her good breeding. I would have hollered something a bit more colorful.

Hit your finger with a hammer? Drive over a parking meter? Lose a bundle with Lehman Brothers? All merit a well-placed swear, in my opinion.

As a lover of words and the English language, I do enjoy a nice round cussword, spoken with gusto and force, with the same relish one might savor a fine Cuban cigar or a glass of Kentucky bourbon (two ice cubes, a little branch). Yes, Mama, I know, I'm on the express train to debauchment. At least I'm in the first-class car where you can swill some decent hooch, smoke tobacco without being burned in effigy, and say "Hot damn!" when the porter brings out a great big hunk of steak.

Unfortunately, what has been lost in our society are the rules and social codification surrounding swearwords. Rules on cussing? Yes, indeed. In the same way a gentleman wouldn't puff his cigar or blow bourbon breath in your face, there should be some general etiquette concerning profanity. The manner marms who carp at cussing are rather silent on the matter. I have a trio of swear rules to live by. So please indulge my elaboration:

Rule #1: Gentlemen don't swear around the fairer sex. Most Southern men learn early on not to swear indiscriminately around their sisters, girlfriends, and wives. It's a lesson usually taught by mothers washing our mouths out with soap. Who came up with that punishment? To this day, I associate the smell of Ivory with some particularly fulsome invective I uttered to my sisters. Believe me, when you have three little sisters, there are plenty of opportunities for Ivory breath. In our house, you wanted Mama to catch you swearing, not Big Daddy. He used Irish Spring, which made Ivory taste, by comparison, like an Oreo.

My first lesson about not cussing in front of women didn't come from a bar of soap, however. It came from Dr. James M. Morgan, Jr., my "Uncle Bubba." Uncle Bubba was a big man, a funny man who enjoyed a joke, and a man who liked the company of other men. Even though he was a surgeon, Dr. Morgan mowed his own grass, oiled his own shotguns, mended his own fences, and occupied himself with the other rituals and pastimes of manhood. I need not tell Southern women this, but when you meet such a man, don't assume he isn't "sensitive." He was a gentle surgeon and a caring person. He just happened to enjoy blasting beavers and other assorted varmints to Kingdom Come.

When I was five years old, Uncle Bubba surgically removed a mole from the back of my neck. Mama and Big Daddy took me to Dr. Morgan's hospital. I took my two stuffed dogs. I recall the mint-green operating room, the bright lights, the nurses in their pretty white uniforms who cooed over me in soothing voices. Then in came Uncle Bubba, "Morgan, my boy!" He was chipper and funny. He told me a joke I still remember: "How do you catch a squirrel, son? Climb up a tree and act like a nut." I thought, well, if he isn't nervous, this can't be that bad.

Before he removed the offending mole, he had to numb the area with an enormous moose shot, right in the neck. He looked at me and said, "Morgan, do you know what to do if it hurts?" I didn't. "Count to ten," he said. So I counted.

"Does it still hurt?" he asked after I'd counted to ten.

"Yes, sir," I mumbled from beneath the two stuffed dogs, which I held over my eyes.

"Do you know what to do if it still hurts?" he asked.

"No sir."

"If it still hurts, swear!" he replied. Then he added, "But

son, we don't swear in front of ladies. Gentlemen don't cuss around girls," and with that, he sent all the nurses out of the operating room.

"Okay boy, have at it," he instructed.

Problem was, I didn't know any cusswords. So Uncle Bubba taught me some.

Boy, what a fiery litany we delivered in that hospital. And lo, it didn't hurt, or at least I don't remember it hurting. This, friends, is why men cuss when we bonk ourselves with lumber, drop golf bags on our feet, or crunch our fingers in the dishwasher. A good swearword satisfies far more than *mercy me* or *lawsy, lawsy* ever could. Thus, no man should ever utter the words *lawsy, lawsy*.

Rule #2: The words. I'm going to use some cusswords here, so look out. The words I employ are not chosen randomly, nor plucked from some schoolyard or dank boiler room. No, my profanity of choice is derived from a divine source. Yep, that's right—all my cussing comes straight out of the Bible.

I believe that if it is in the Bible, you can say it. Period. Fortunately for me, that opens up a whole range of blasphemy. Think about it. Every other page in the Old Testament, some poor sap is getting damned somewhere, usually to hell. Loose women and fatherless children abound. People ride asses all over the place. And I'm quite certain that *somfabitch* is in there somewhere. I just haven't found it yet.

The problem with these words is that they just don't really have much shock value anymore. Old Gilbert and Sullivan were making fun of society's objection to the curse "damne" in *H.M.S. Pinafore*, written in 1878. It didn't make audiences swoon back then, and it doesn't now.

So to get by on these old words, one must use them creatively, lest they simply fall flat among the cacophony of modern vulgarity. Which brings me to:

Rule #3: Usage. How one swears is just as important in the overall impact as what one actually swears. Some people are mutterers. Others curse under their breath. Still more erupt in small torrents of hisses, like deflating tires. These are all wrong, I tell you, wrong.

A swear should be affirmatively and strongly delivered, the verbal cousin to a handshake. Swear 'em right in the eye. No mealy-mouthed vulgarians need apply.

Of course, given the right circumstance, all three of these rules may be smashed into oblivion. I'll leave you with the example of my great-grandmother, a lovely and stern pillar of society. She invited a group of ladies over to her house in Montgomery one spring afternoon fifty years ago. Mrs. Wiggins maintained a fine home, decorated with English antiques. As she came out of the foyer and into her living room to greet the assembled bridge club, she strode across a Persian prayer rug, which in the South we call a *throw rug*. There's a reason we call it that. I should add here that my dear great-grandmother was a "sturdy" woman, which magnified the force at which that rug catapulted her onto a Chippendale coffee table. By the time she, the rug, and the table hit the floor, there wasn't enough intact wood left to pick your teeth with. What to do? Swear.

Great-grandmother lifted herself up, dusted off her dress, and said, "Damn, I liked that coffee table."

Entirely appropriate, I think, don't you?

How to Upbraid a Person

It is possible to lay into someone with grace and good manners. And since these moments are usually far more interesting to others than our day-to-day modus operandi, it is doubly as important to exude control, intelligence, and a grasp of what I call "conflict etiquette."

Never insult people you don't know. They could be dangerous. They might be your future boss. And most of the time, the ones we most want to insult, we already know anyway—as one has to know a person in order to truly dislike them.

Never insult an easy target. It's unbecoming. The exempt include your employees, surly toll-booth operators, customer service representatives, makeup-counter girls, grocery store bag boys, and all manner of government civil servants (and no, you can't cuss the clerk at the P.O.).

This is critical to your success as a thoroughbred belittler: do not raise your voice. You're not P.T. Barnum. Yelling shows a lack of control, and maintaining great volume usually attracts unwanted attention, in addition to making your face look blotchy.

Finally, end your parry and jab as quickly as possible, lest you be subtly upbraided as a visitor of Jane Austen's once was: "You have delighted us long enough."

Chapter 6

Southern Semantics

Fine with Me

Southern women do not always say exactly what they mean. We're not hard to translate—unless you're not from around here. It's a cultural thing. In truth, it helps to be a native speaker no matter where you live. The local patois is always a little different. It takes years of living in the South, marinating in the heat and the humidity, to appreciate all the nuances of our language. Most importantly, you have to consider context. While this is true for the rest of the country, too, I like to think of us down here as a little bit special. I mean that in the unique, delightful, charming way rather than the Special Olympics, mentally challenged definition.

The words being uttered are often less important than the people involved or the timing of the remarks. For example, if a couple in the South has a mixed marriage, an Alabama fan and an Auburn fan living under the same roof, then Iron Bowl week can get dicey. One spouse might scream at the other, "I want a divorce!" I wouldn't pay nearly as much attention to that comment during Iron Bowl week as I would during any other time of the year. I understand that these things happen. Divorce demands arising from stressful football weeks in the

Southeastern Conference seem, to me, to be an entirely understandable and even predictable turn of events.

We have all said things in the heat of the moment that we don't really mean and would not dream of saying on any other day. Although I do not remember this myself, my husband claims that I told him and a labor-and-delivery nurse to shut up during one of my children's births. That is pretty strong language. Saying "shut up" to another human being in this house costs you five dollars, the equivalent of a large caffe latte. I remember thinking those words in my head, but I don't remember saying them out loud. I can't say for sure that I didn't let a "shut up" slip out. Childbirth is one of those stressful circumstances I was talking about.

I've found that it pays to wait until the dust settles, the campaign ends, the football season is over, or the baby goes to college to address some issues. I take into account extenuating circumstances—like in-laws camped out in the guest room, the challenges of a new weight-loss diet, or recent changes in medication—before I take to heart any offending comments from someone I love. Lord knows, I certainly hope that people who love me take into account recent "take to my bed with a cold cloth on my forehead" provocations in my own life before judging any hasty words that have flown out of my mouth without a filtering review by my brain.

One word that is found in every Southern woman's lexicon strikes me as particularly in need of cultural translation: the F-word. No need to panic. This essay is G-rated. I have a good vocabulary and Internet access to every dictionary on the planet. I don't need to stoop that low for entertainment. As the mother of teenage boys, if I want humor on the scale of bathroom jokes, I can fill up my cup on the home front.

At first glance, the word *fine* seems pretty innocuous. Nevertheless, I believe that there is not a more loaded word in a Southern woman's vocabulary. I promise you that the more you think about this word, the more meanings you will divine. If this word appeared in a Southerner's dictionary, the definitions would spill onto two pages and require full-color illustrations.

At first glance, *fine* can mean anything. It all depends on your tone of voice. It can mean something straightforward, such as a response to a question regarding someone's physical or mental well-being. One might ask, for example, "Are you okay?" A response of, "Fine! I survived the fall from the balcony!" is easy to translate. This definition for *fine* is just the first round of rush parties, however. There are days and days of parties to get through before you select a *fine* that is the perfect match.

Think about this: The first question we all ask someone who has sustained an injury is, "Are you okay?" This frequently causes irritation because, by definition, the person who has just banged his or her head on the car door, fallen off the edge of the roof, or been struck by a rattlesnake is clearly anything *but* fine. In fact, every accident victim is the exact opposite of fine.

This Q-and-A interchange is a cultural reflex. The "Are you okay?" query is actually a plea for reassurance that the injured party is still breathing. We figure if the injured party can articulate a polite response, it can't be all that bad. It sounds more polite to ask, "Are you okay?" rather than "Are you maimed for life?" or "Are your brains splattered on the sidewalk?" or "I guess that's the last time you'll poke a snake with a stick; isn't it?"

Down here, the only socially acceptable answer to "Are you okay?" is "I'm fine." You can see how important tone becomes with this word. You can say "fine" in a sarcastic, ticked-off, "Why are you asking me such a stupid question?" way, or you can reply "fine" in a breathy, "I'm just about to breathe my last breath on earth; come close and I'll tell you where I hid the money" way. It depends.

It is possible to use the word *fine* to actually reassure others, as in, "I'm fine in the assisted-living facility. I play bridge on Thursdays; the food here is fabulous, and they have fresh flowers and linen tablecloths in the dining room. I should have moved in here years ago. I have no idea why I waited until I broke my hip to get in on this deal." In this context, the meaning is clearly reassuring. Conversely, you can use the word *fine* to make your loved ones feel as guilty as if they have drowned a basketful of kittens—as in, "I'm fine here in this nursing home. I could die tomorrow, and no one would know for two weeks until I started to smell up the place." See how this works?

You often hear the word *fine* shouted in angry tones: "That is perfectly fine with me!" The quick translation, down and dirty, for this is: "I don't care if I ever see you or speak to you again as long as I live!" You've probably used this application of the word yourself. It's a classic. My guess is that this is actually the most common use of the F-word.

Sometimes, the word *fine* really means fine, and you shouldn't read anything oxymoronic into it at all. It can be an automatic response to a general greeting in the South. One might ask, "Hey! How're you doing?" The answer, as any Southerner over the age of five can tell you, is "Fine, thanks. How are you?" This can go back and forth for a while. It's compulsory, really, a knee-jerk, polite greeting, ingrained from an early age as a sign of good manners. You should know that this *fine* does not necessarily reflect reality in any literal way. It would not shock me to hear a conversation like this:

"Hey, how's your family?"

"Oh, we're all fine. Mama was sick for a while, but she's perking up. How're y'all?"

"We're fine, too, thanks."

The last line could easily be followed, mere seconds later, by, "I think that is the tornado siren. If we don't get down in the basement, I think we're going to be on the five o'clock news."

Even a seemingly transparent use of the word *fine* can be misleading. Picture this scene in your mind: A doctor goes into an exam room to treat a Southern woman with the flu. She is throwing up in the trash can usually reserved for wadded-up paper gowns. This woman fears she may expire at any moment. Considering how ill she feels, she thinks death may not be such a bad idea.

The doctor asks, in his or her best bedside-manner voice, "So, how're you, Ms. —?"

Before she even lifts her head from the trash can to answer that stupid question in colorful detail, she'll say—you guessed it, I'm sure—"I'm fine."

Don't worry. She'll get to the "fine, *but* . . ." part pretty fast.

It wouldn't surprise me a bit to hear paramedics going through the traditional meet-and-greet ritual with a victim they are trying to free from the twisted wreck of a car with the Jaws of Life. The word *fine* has elaborate, complex, multi-layered, and strangely fascinating meanings in our culture. It would make an interesting doctoral dissertation. I'd read it. On second thought, I think I could write it. I've spent a life-time researching the topic.

Decoding Southern Women

If you understood Melinda's essay on the language of Southern femininity, your X chromosomes are in place. As a man, there exist some nuances of life that I have resigned myself to missing: (a) childbirth, (b) setting a table properly, and (c) grasping what Southern women mean when they talk to me.

Sure, I comprehend the words that Southern women utter. I'm just never quite sure I have a command of what they mean. Exhibit A: it took Melinda four pages to explain one word, *fine*, and the next time she employs that word in my company, I will mentally rewind her exhaustive explanation of *fine*, mulling over the myriad different potential meanings, and try to parse exactly which definition is the one that she actually means.

Men, you know my likelihood of success: probably zero.

Not that I haven't made an earnest effort to understand women, mind you. I have three sisters. Four of my bosses were women. Many of my friends are women. I listen. I study. I struggle to understand.

It's futile.

This isn't to say that Southern men aren't derogatory, insulting, and sarcastic at times. Difference is, most of the time you know if you're the subject of a man's ire. A Southern man's insults hit you like a Greyhound bus. Wham! You're obliterated. A Southern woman's insults are like seeing a shooting star, "Hey, was that a shooting star over there? I think it was." You're never quite certain you've been insulted, and you need someone else to verify what you heard.

Oh, my good man, you think you understand Southern women? That you're the male exception? You're that blind pig that finds an acorn every now and then? Okay, here's a test: when your wife/mother/girlfriend/sister says, "I'm fine, really," after an argument, what does she mean?

Perhaps a lightbulb went off in your head and you thought, "She's not fine; she's furious."

Good job. You've passed one-hundredth of the test. You've glimpsed into the enigma machine and gleamed a nuance. Now what? What are you going to do with that information? The woman is angry with you; now you know that she is angry with you, and you know that she's trying to pretend she's not angry with you. Question: does she know you know she's furious? Should you let on that you know? Does she want you to know she's angry but still get credit for being "fine"? If you let on that you know she's not fine, will she be angrier? Is she saying she's fine because she wants to make up or because she wants you to feel guilty and show remorse? Does she want sympathy? Pity? Groveling? Is she frustrated? How do you know?

You don't know, Jack. Stop pretending that you do.

We men don't know if you women are fascinated or bored silly when you say, "How interesting. . . ." We're not sure if you like somebody or hate her when you say, "Bless her heart." We don't know whether to run away or put on some mood music when you say, "Now just what do you think you're doing, mister?"

We men are all just gamblers at the verbal roulette table of Southern women. And the truth is: we like it like that.

When I was single, I took an ad out in the *Andalusia Star-News* that read: "Wanted: S. Belle. Only polite but fiery, willful but fragile, dewy but tough, flirtatious yet innocent, beautiful but dangerous-to-touch candidates need apply. Female is a must. Will enjoy Southern gentleman, lifelong supply of

MoonPies, and a crazy set of in-laws."

It didn't work. No Southern woman (at that time) would ever place a telephone call to a man.

Southern men like the excitement of ambiguity. We like the hunt. We bore easily, and as a result, the women of the South have created an entire language of mystery to keep us guessing.

Like bass to a shiny lure, we men spend all this time trying to understand what women mean. It's as futile as looking heavenward on an evening stroll and trying to grasp the universe, time, or space. Leave that to the professionals with bigger telescopes.

What Southern males need is our own verbal armor, our own lexicon of subterfuge. Problem is, we're just too straightforward. When a man says, "He's a friend of mine," that means he's a friend. We'll be buddies with just about anybody, provided they don't try to run off with our wives or businesses. When a man says, "He's an ass," the guy in question could give rides at the Grand Canyon. If he says, "I'm sorry," he's really sorry. Sorry he made you mad. Sorry he's standing there saying he's sorry. Sorry he's so sorry. When a Southern man says, "I love you," look out. He loves you. Loves every inch of you. Loves you like a summer nap, his mama, or a day watching his favorite football team.

Think I'm wrong, fellow? Go ahead and try your own coded version of the language. Good luck with that. Women know men are simple beasts. They've got us figured out. Try and practice their own dark alchemy on them, and you'll scramble the airwaves.

The man who says, "Your mother is such a *delight*," isn't fooling anybody.

If a man says, "She's got a great *personality*!" she knows you think she's fat.

It's not a term of affection when you say, "*Honey*, I said the game was tonight, not tomorrow." The *honey* doesn't sweeten the message.

Far better, gentlemen, to stick to the basics. Say what you mean and mean what you say, and we'll all be just *fine*.

Chapter 7

Hoarding

Save That for Me

Southern women are savers. I think it comes from necessary accommodations to hard times. Generations of women have learned to make do. They pass down household tricks of the trade used to successfully steer hungry families through the lean years. Some things we save make sense. Other things we accumulate have no rhyme or reason. The saving compulsion can get a little squirrelly. Who knows what we may need in the future? It's best not to throw anything away, we reason.

Whenever I flip television channels with the remote control and stumble across a mama bird wrestling a juicy worm from the ground to drop into a nest full of wide-open baby beaks, I feel a connection. I know how that mama bird feels. Someone is always hungry around here, too. I swear there hasn't been a cold skillet in this house in a decade. Mamas are mamas—regardless of their species—and they will do anything to feed their offspring.

What I've discovered about Southern mamas is that there is a compulsion to save deeply ingrained in each of us. When a Southern baby girl is born, I think an angel pauses on the baby assembly line and says, "I see this one's headed down South.

I'm going to need an extra handful of 'saving' dust for this baby. She's going to have to keep up with a lot of silver," she tells the rest of the heavenly host.

Many of us Southerners live in old houses where closet space is at a premium. Nevertheless, valuable storage space is routinely devoted to empty boxes. That's right. Not a birthday, Christmas, graduation, or wedding goes by without admonitions from female relatives to the honoree to "Save that box! It's a good one!" The Save the Whales crowd has nothing on a Southern woman intent on preserving a good box. She will hang over a present before you can untie the bow, like a vulture waiting to pounce on a fresh carcass. It's hard for her to restrain herself. She feels the need to supervise your unwrapping to protect a box's future potential.

Environmentalists would approve of Southern box-savers. Everything is all about reusing now. We Southern women are ahead of our time in so many ways. It is sad for me to note how often our gifts to the world go unappreciated.

Another product we Southern women can't resist hoarding like squirrels with an obsessive-compulsive disorder is aluminum foil. Have you ever thought about all the things you can do with tinfoil? Every Southern woman I know has a drawer crammed with leftover tinfoil. I don't care what those professional chefs say; you can reuse tinfoil. I've done it. My mother does it. My grandmother did it, and we haven't killed anybody yet. Well . . . no one's ever *proved* any of us contributed, directly or indirectly, to the death of anyone. That's my point. I think we can all agree on that.

Of course, you have to use common sense in saving. You don't reuse tinfoil that has icing stuck to it. Getting that off would be way too much work. It's the equivalent of washing plastic spoons and forks. Women who do that are way too cheap to shop with the rest of us. God made plastic utensils for a reason. It is understood that there are minimum sanitary standards that should trump our innate thriftiness. You don't reuse tinfoil if you've covered meat marinating for the grill with it. We all know about cross-contamination. No one wants to be remembered as the woman who brought the salmonella casserole to the mommy and her brand-new baby, causing them to spend their first twenty-four hours together on earth stretched out on the bathroom floor.

On the other hand, if all that tinfoil has ever done is cover up some hot rolls, you better believe it's going to get reused. That's just being a good steward of our natural resources. (Is tinfoil a natural resource? I don't know a thing about aluminum, except that you can recycle aluminum cans. Don't e-mail me with the answer, either. Honestly, I don't really care.) Best of all, reusing aluminum foil saves money in the family grocery budget. If saving a bit on tinfoil will help send one of my children to college, then it will have been worth it. Every little bit helps. It makes me feel virtuous to be a tinfoil saver. It's a matter of civic pride, one of the small ways I can help save the planet.

As a short aside, let me remind you that pennies really do add up. My kids go to a camp every summer called Camp McDowell. The camp was built with pennies collected in Episcopal parishes all over Alabama after World War II. I don't understand why everyone is so contemptuous about pennies. Most adults are too important to reach down and pick up a penny. I think that says something about our society, and it isn't anything good.

Have you ever tried to cash in a big jar of pennies at the bank? The bank tellers act like you are trying to shove a pickle jar full of cow patties through the window instead of ten years' worth of change salvaged from pants' pockets so it won't tear up the washing machine. Banks should be all about pennies; don't you agree? I think banks have some nerve being snotty about small-change deposits. If I were running a bank, I'd be out on the sidewalk hawking for pennies with a megaphone. "Citizens! No change too small for this bank! Pennies, dimes, nickels—we'll take whatever you've got!"

Now that I got that out of my system, back to tinfoil.

My favorite sentimental use for tinfoil happened years ago when my kids made star ornaments for the Christmas tree. One child always bloodied a finger trying to tear the tinfoil on the serrated edge of the box. Tinfoil stars remind me of my favorite short story in the whole world, Truman Capote's "A Christmas Memory." (If you've never read that, don't let the sun go down until you do that today. You'll thank me for it.) I let my kids use the whole drawer full of leftovers because Christmas is not the time for being stingy with tinfoil.

I just heard a story about a man who paid to store all his parents' household goods for a couple of years after their deaths until he could bear to sort through a lifetime of this-and-that and make rational decisions about what to do with it all. When he finally opened the boxes, guess what he found inside? Mayonnaise jars. That's right. He'd been paying to store empty mayo jars. I can see how that could happen. Mayo jars are good for almost everything.

You can throw away grease you used to fry speckled trout caught in Apalachicola Bay in mayo jars. (One does not reuse fish grease, just in case you are not from the South, and your mama didn't teach you that.) I did that just last night.

You can use those jars to take homemade soup to sick people. I did that this week, too. One jar holds enough soup for two people unless one person is a real pig. With the unpretentious mayo jar, no one has to return the container to you. I believe that it is mean to take a sick or grieving person baked goods on a plate you are going to get worked up over getting back. One of the first things Southern women do when a loved one dies is dig up a roll of masking tape from the kitchen junk drawer and find a pad of paper to record the food offerings which are about to pour in. We all want to return platters, tins, and bowls to their rightful owners, yet every funeral results in a few mystery platters whose owners cannot be identified. Since the world as we know it may stop spinning on its axis if a thank-you note doesn't arrive in short order raving over the specifics of Miss so-and-so's spiced-peach congealed salad, which, no doubt, has unique restorative powers for the recently bereaved, you can see why the masking tape and the list are so important.

Sick-people soup is not the final word on the many uses of the mayo jar. You can punch holes in the lid and use a mayo jar to catch lightning bugs. Be careful punching those holes. You'd be amazed at how much damage an ice pick can do to the human hand. My kids used to catch lightning bugs a lot. There was an incident. I'm pretty sure it was an accident. What's done is done. Let's just leave it at that.

I even heard of one other use for mayo jars on long car trips, but that one is a bit too indelicate to share. Use your imagination. You'll get there.

Of course, you can use mayo jars to store leftovers. My kids have learned to dread the sight of last night's leftovers in the mayo jar because they know that I am not above adding the leftovers to everyone's scrambled eggs the next morning. This works well with shrimp, bacon, sausage, even pork tenderloin, and all sorts of vegetables like onions, tomatoes, and peppers. I freely admit that adding the leftover tuna was a mistake. I stand by my premise, however. Waste not; want not.

My favorite hoarding story is about my friend Laura's mother. (SWAG readers will recognize the name Laura. She appears in all my books, as do many of my friends. I really don't get out that much.) Laura's mother lives in Montgomery, Alabama, and she is a fairly typical saver of her generation. Her particular foible is florists' vases. She can't bear to throw them away. She's a gifted flower arranger, and she frequently takes bouquets to others, so she NEEDS those vases. One problem: she ran out of storage space. So, she called up a company and ordered one of those storage units you put behind your house. Pretty soon, she filled that up, too. Another storage unit soon joined the first out back. You can see where I'm going with this. When her daughter asked her what she was going to do about all the vases, she remained unfazed. "I'm not going to do anything about it," she said. "Those vases are going to be your problem after I'm gone." You have to admire her solution to the clean-out problem. I find her inspirational.

At some point in every Southern woman's life, she has been forced by the vicissitudes of her circumstances to feed the masses in her dining room with the proverbial loaves and fishes. Her mother, grandmother, and great-grandmother undoubtedly had to do the same thing at some point in their lives. The rest of you out there who get presents in the "good" boxes that have been reused since the Clinton administration, or those of you who are recipients of homemade soup in mayo jars, or you lucky few who get the tinfoil-covered pound cakes better be appreciative. If it weren't for us Southern savers, there'd be nothing left for the rest of you.

Ten Things Every Woman Saves

Ponytail holders. In households with girls, there are thousands of these in every drawer like crash carts on cardiac units.

Rubber bands. Specifically, the purple rubber bands used to hold the asparagus stalks together from the grocery store.

Cards and letters. You never know who you might need to blackmail in the future.

Hotel toiletries. Swiping hotel toiletries isn't stealing. Think of them as party favors.

Miniature liquor bottles. They're inexplicably appealing and often lead to dangerous hotel room trips around the world.

Church bulletins. These pile up until you can't remember why you saved them in the first place.

Tissue paper, wrapping paper, and bags. These can be reused until they eventually return to the original purchaser.

Makeup samples. Even if they're totally wrong for us, we can't throw them away because they were FREE.

Coupons. Even if it is twenty percent off the price of a casket, we save it because *you never know*.

Cash. A private slush fund in a woman's underwear drawer is always a wise investment.

A Penny Saved Is a Cent

When a Southern woman saves something, it's considered thrifty, wise, and altogether smart thinking. When a Southern man saves something, it's considered useless, compulsive, and bordering on hoarding disease.

My mother saves grease from her skillet. This is deemed normal in the South, and in some households, healthy. The coffee can of grease has been beneath my mother's kitchen sink since 1968. I'm not kidding. It sits safely between the bleach, furniture polish, bug killer, and radioactive substance Mama uses to polish the silver. (A Southern woman's silver must be gleaming, no matter what the consequences may be for the environment and the people who eat off of it.) Although I admit that sludge tastes fabulous, it cannot be good for you to eat grease from bacon cooked in the Johnson administration. Not to mention it has been lingering next to DDT and other household chemicals for five decades. Still, pillars of Southern society warmly regard this practice to be *smart saving.*

Men: try pulling out the venison meat you've saved from a hunt back in 1985 and see if any woman, anywhere, will consume it. I think not. That venison is considered a waste of freezer space—something to be thrown out in favor of Ben & Jerry's or a lasagna Lean Cuisine.

Men save things out of two motives: (1) anticipation of disaster and (2) because, deep down, we're sentimental. The first category includes items such as bullets, which we hoard in case the black helicopters come for our families. (As a child, I never worried that the Soviets would invade Alabama. It would have been open season, i.e., "Hey Bubba, we got us another Russkie on the bypass!") We save rations in case of a bad storm. We save cans of Freon and one-hundred-watt lightbulbs because someone told us we couldn't. (If you don't think a flickering compact florescent doesn't count as an emergency, you haven't had to wait for one to warm up while you thought you had a household intruder at 2:00 a.m.)

In the sentimental category, we save easy chairs we bought for our first apartment (hey, they're comfy), lucky sports shirts, savings bonds from our grandmothers, childhood baseball cards (they're worth a fortune, really), and love letters from you.

If that's clutter, so be it. Every house needs a touch of humanity.

Now, saving money is another story. I believe Ben Franklin was an idiot. Funny britches and stringy hair aside, he just didn't know what he was talking about.

The man wanted the turkey to be the national bird. The turkey.

He also said, "A penny saved is a penny earned." What a moron. Granted, up until this week, I actually believed the old coot. If I saw a penny on the ground while walking down the street, I would actually stoop over and pick it up, in complete disregard of my personal safety (a penny can be covered in germs—you never know how many small children have digested it).

For years, I have saved every penny, nickel, dime, and quarter. I have mayonnaise jars that sit in my kitchen, proudly holding my booty. And every night, cha-chink, I throw in my change from the day. After a few months, I roll said change, haul it down to a building with a sign that says BANK and exchange it for larger bills (I find it embarrassing to pay for dinner with rolls of pennies), preferably with ole Ben Franklin on the face.

Last Monday morning, I decided to roll up my coins to take to the "bank." It took two hours to roll up the moolah, but when I was done, I had $73.87, which felt like free money.

I went to no fewer than three banks in my neighborhood. I won't name names, but let's just say they were banks with signs like, "We Love Our Customers!" and "Our Customers Come First!" or "Service Is Our Priority!" In each bank, the response was the same. You would have thought I was trying to exchange live chickens for twenty-dollar bills instead of American money. Cold hard cash for crumpled green cash. What could be easier? But in modern banking, one must have an account at the bank and write your name, address, and account number on each roll before they will make a swap with you. These are banks that spend millions promoting their stupendous customer service with features like online banking, teller banking, touch-tone banking, PC banking, free checking, checkless checking, electronic checking, twenty-four-hour checking, debit cards, teller cards, automated teller machines, and even coffee in the lobby. But they don't change money, which technically costs nothing.

A little banking history: the word *bank* comes from the French word *banq*, which means *bench*. If you go to Chartres Cathedral in Chartres, France, you'll see a stained-glass window with all these medieval folk sitting on benches counting out money. Each town in the Middle Ages had its own currency, so if you went from Paris to Chartres, you needed to visit the money changers who sat on *banques*. Modern banking, you see, sprang up from exchanging money—for example, coins for bills.

Banks lost hundreds of millions in robberies and check fraud last year. They wrote down billions in bad assets. Many are teetering on financial insolvency. Yet they act like swapping pennies is the one act that will push them over the brink and literally break the bank. Banking has fallen off its bench.

So I went to the grocery store. I figured I'd just buy some groceries with all my rolled coins. The store was willing to accept my American Express but not my American nickels. So then I went to the dry cleaners. They didn't take a dime. Finally, I went to the post office. I figured that the bastion of bureaucracy, the only place of business in America where you can actually buy something for a cent, the good old P.O., would accept my money. They even had a sign in the window that said, "Pay Any Way," meaning that they accepted MasterCard, Visa, Diners Club, etcetera. They didn't accept the coinage. I almost went postal.

So there I was, standing with thirty pounds of groceries, three sheets of stamps, my dry cleaning, and what was beginning to feel like ten tons of coins. I was a bitter, bitter man.

I decided to take my complaint to THE UNITED STATES FEDERAL RESERVE. No little two-hour drive to Atlanta was going to stop me from trading my coins for some tender I could actually use. I figured that they'd accept my bling since they minted them in the first place (and a penny costs more to make than it is worth). After winding my way through the metal detectors and into the heart of the reserve (I guess they're afraid someone might nickel and dime them to death), I filled out the necessary paperwork and placed my rolled $73.87 into the vault. The frumpy man behind the glass said, "You'll have to unroll those, Mr. Murphy." With the gas money I spent on the trip, getting rid of those coins only cost me $42.66.

So now, yes, I step over coins in the street.

Chapter 8

That Twinkle in Your Eye

All That Glitters

Men like shiny things. They like race cars and yard tools and golf clubs. Quite a few men like to collect shiny things, like old coins. When my sons were young, they loved to plunge their hands into piles of Mardi Gras doubloons. One of the most fun birthday parties we ever had at our house involved a search for pirate treasure (a bag of silver dollars) in the monkey grass in our backyard. Following the treasure map with its singed edges and X-marks-the-spot directions proved irresistible to four-year-old males.

You know what else likes shiny things? Raccoons. That's right. Raccoons have been known to make off with all sorts of human plunder—things like car keys, sunglasses, and even jewelry. I can tell you right now that if a raccoon swiped my favorite gold bangle, I'd know just what to do about it. I'd round up some male friends, tell them to bring their shiny shotguns, and show them which way the critter fled. I love nature as much as the next woman, but if the choice is between my diamond earrings and a raccoon, I say shoot that sucker quick, before he climbs a tree and gets away. Although I would prefer not to shoot it myself, I feel certain I would be able to supervise the endeavor quite easily. Bossing comes naturally to all the women in my family, including me. I would aid and abet any man willing to do the dirty deed for me. I don't care a thing about raccoons, and if shooting a raccoon isn't a job for a Southern man, then I don't know what is.

Southern women like shiny things, too. Jewelry is shiny. It's sparkly, too. Generally, the more it sparkles, the more we like it. You should know, however, that there is a wide spectrum of personal taste with regard to shiny jewelry selection. It pays to check with the Southern woman you plan to adorn. It is better to be safe rather than sorry when you are buying by the carat. More expensive is not necessarily better. If you are buying for me, I like elegant and simple; think Audrey Hepburn. But I have friends who prefer the Zsa Zsa Gabor approach to diamonds. I can take or leave diamonds, but I will flat drop some cash on pearls in any shape, size, or design. I never saw a string of pearls I didn't want to try on. You should not take my pearls-over-diamonds preference as gospel for all Southern women, however. I am a rarity in so many ways.

Every Southern girl needs these jewelry staples: long pearls to wear to everything from rush parties to any other event for the rest of her life; short pearls to get married in and pass down to her daughter; monogrammed gold bangles—it's always nice to have choices; pearl earrings; diamond earrings; a good cameo; and at least one unique (preferably antique) piece of jewelry—a brooch, ring, buyer's choice—to commemorate the birth of each child. Every Southern man should have enough sense to know that a woman who spends nine months carrying his child around in her uterus and then twenty-seven hours pushing it out into the world deserves a little treat from the jewelry store. Nothing says thank you to a Southern woman better than a big piece of jewelry. Now that I think about it, nothing says, "I'm sorry," "My mother was wrong about you," "Happy Birthday," or "I'd marry you again in a heartbeat" better, either.

Some men are just plain gifted at picking out jewelry that we women actually want to wear. Usually, this is because they have been raised right by a generation or two of Southern women. (Yes, yes, it should be *reared*. It's a Southern colloquialism. Deal with it.) My friend's husband, Jim, is good at picking out jewelry for her. In addition, he has the good sense to bring his gift selections to my house for my approval before he gives them to his wife. I am just pleased as punch to help him choose the best thing because I always know what it is. As an added bonus, I get to try on the jewelry and play dress-up for a few minutes while I decide what he'd like to give his wife. This is a win-win jewelry selection process if I ever saw one.

Unfortunately, a lot of men are sadly lacking in picking-out talent. Sometimes, they seem attracted to the ugliest designs imaginable—earrings that look like weapons or something you would hang from a Christmas tree or pendants that look like they could double as toe tags for the county morgue. Sadly, spending a lot of money does not guarantee one jewelry-selection success. Remember that jewelers have to stock some tacky pieces for buyers who have bad taste. This is one of life's little tragedies even if it does make good business sense.

If you look hard enough, you can find tacky jewelry in Tiffany and Company. I know a man who somehow managed to do that. He bought his grown-up wife a snowman slide bracelet for Christmas. It was even worse in real life than you are imagining it right now. How disappointed would you be to open Tiffany's signature, light-blue box to find a snowman bracelet inside?

You have to be careful with the whole shiny package attractiveness. I have a theory that our reactions to shiny things are a result of our innate, genetic programming. You know how deadly flora and fauna lure unsuspecting animals to their deaths? Picture a vibrantly colored, deadly plant in the rainforest. Imagine it loaded with tasty pollen. The second an unsuspecting insect lands on a leaf, WHAM! The insect gets gobbled up by a carnivorous plant that is slightly higher on the food chain. Mother Nature is not for the squeamish.

You'd think with all the nature-worshiping most men indulge in with hunting, fishing, golfing, and other outdoor activities that make me hot even to think about, that men would be wise to the dangers of shiny, attractive packaging, but I see them falling for the same superficial, shiny, looks-good-on-the-outside packages in women all the time. If you put a good-looking hooker in some shiny jewelry, there's not a man in the world who won't give her a second glance. I'm not suggesting he's going to take it any further than that, necessarily, but he'll still window-shop pretty hard.

In the end, I guess, men aren't that different from raccoons. They see a shiny thing. They want it. They grab it and run off with it if they can. Often times, they don't know what to do with it once they get it. I read that raccoons like to dunk their treasures over and over in water. I guess we should thank our lucky stars that men don't do that with the shiny women they throw over their shoulders and take home to their man caves. I don't know a woman in the world who would like to be dunked over and over in a river. I think they tried that once in Salem. It didn't work out too well back then, either.

Morgan Murphy
Shiny Things

Mama's jewelry box held a silver whistle in the shape of a butterfly. When I was about eighteen months old, she found me playing with that butterfly, and I uttered some of my first words: "shiny things." She said later that she felt sorry for me because she thought I'd never own shiny things like her jewelry.

She was right in the respect that I'd never own a lot of flashy bling. Some men do wear a prodigious amount of jewelry, but as I have no mafia connections, have never won a Super Bowl, and have little rap experience outside of playing the Modern Major General in *Pirates of Penzance*, I limit my flash to a wedding band, signet ring, and watch.

Men like me may be understated in their jewelry but nonetheless express their love of shiny things in other ways. We love chrome-laden cars and polished titanium golf clubs. Shimmering aluminum computers and stereo equipment holds a special place in our brains. We like sparkly bass boats and engraved shotguns. From brass fittings to highly lacquered woodworking, if we can put a gleam on it, we do.

Men love shimmer. Judas betrayed Christ for what? Oh yeah, thirty pieces of silver. And I'll bet that apple Eve handed

Adam had a pretty good gleam on it. We men are suckers for gleam. Even the burliest, most grizzled man's man is transfixed by glitter. Men like that invaded California for the gold rush. You can see them in the old pictures from San Francisco in the 1800s: beard down to the navel, tattered work gear, pickax in one hand, glimmering nugget in the other—giant, toothless smile. Men sailed around the world in search of twinkling treasure. We've been smashing each other upside the head for hundreds of years on quests for pearls, platinum, diamonds, rubies, and emeralds. We adore shiny things.

Women know this about us, of course, and exploit our weakness for a little razzle-dazzle with coruscation of every sort: lip gloss, hair conditioner, glittering blush, twinkling eye shadow, extra-long-lasting-shimmering-eyelash-extending mascara, sequined dresses, rhinestone-encrusted accessories, even shimmery panty hose. When Mrs. Murphy slinks into my highly polished 1958 Eldorado with her shiny hair, shiny eyes, shiny lips, and shiny legs, well, friends, the gleam in my eye isn't just a trick of the light. Vroom.

Given this adoration of all things gleaming, I cannot overemphasize the importance of a man knowing a good jeweler. My jeweler is Sperry Snow, the owner of Barton-Clay Jewelers. When I was very broke, living in New York, Sperry used to take me to dinner whenever he came to buy diamonds. I undoubtedly ranked as his worst client (I usually bought fifty dollars worth of modest Christmas presents from his Birmingham store every year). Yet, Sperry and his diamond brokers treated me like their biggest spender, with meals that would have made Solomon blush, at spots such as Mr. Chow's, 21, and Le Cirque. Times like those always made me wish my appendix worked.

Unfortunately for Sperry, when the time came to propose to Mrs. Murphy, I really didn't need a ring. Like many Southern fellows, I'd been given my grandmother's wedding band and engagement ring for that very purpose. My mother's mother had been a war bride, circa 1941, and though her engagement ring's setting was incredibly elaborate and beautiful, the stone itself had a slight, almost imperceptible inclusion. I felt more than a little guilty about not needing to purchase an engagement ring from Sperry, so I took Grandmother's ring to his posh store and asked him to take a look at replacing the diamond. Nervous groom-to-be, I wanted everything to be perfect and was ready to buy a new stone for the old ring. Sperry listened for a moment, took out his jeweler's loop, and peered at the glittering stone my grandmother wore for fifty-two years. He paused and said, "Morgan, any woman that doesn't appreciate this ring just as it is doesn't deserve to wear it. If you want to change the diamond, you'll have to go elsewhere."

Now that's a friend. I, of course, didn't change the stone, and Mrs. Murphy adores the engagement ring and all the family history to which it bears witness.

The story doesn't end there, however. Since I didn't have to purchase an engagement ring or a wedding band, I had a little cash left over to buy Mrs. Murphy a wedding gift. Naturally, I paid a visit to Sperry's store, determined to buy something, anything, from the man who had been so generous to me for all those years. I planned to buy a small cross necklace or perhaps a nice pair of earrings, and I took my mother along for consulting purposes. We shopped and shopped, as I weighed the individual merits of a few modest pieces in the case.

While I debated which gift might be best for the soon-to-be Mrs. Murphy, Mama spotted a big, honking, call-your-broker-and-liquidate-your-401(k) sapphire ring, encircled by diamonds. She had the salesgirl bring it out, and we had a laugh for a moment or two about my buying it. "Go big or go home," the salesgirl said, and we all three fell out into hysterics.

While we were still laughing, an old girlfriend suddenly slithered into the store. Gentle readers, this is a girl who broke my heart and worse—she took my dog. (Never take a Southern man's hound. That's low.) The faint odor of sulfur followed. My mother's eyes narrowed. The devil sauntered up in a pale-blue sundress and purred, "My, my, Morgan, what are you doing here?"

"Oh not much, really," I lied, gesturing casually at the sapphire boulder on the display counter, "just buying this little wedding present for my fiancée."

Shallow? Yes. Completely juvenile behavior? Absolutely. Bitter? Party of one, present. Worth the six months it took to pay for it?

You bet.

To this day, Mrs. Murphy gets a certain twinkle in her eye every time someone compliments her shiny, blue ring.

Chapter 9

Valentine's Day

Construction-Paper
Hearts

I love Valentine's Day. I love every single thing about it. I love the romance of it. I love that the holiday excludes extended family members. I love that it doesn't require decorations. I love that I don't have to spend big money on my valentine (although if you can do so without eating chicken noodle soup for a month, and you are so inclined, then don't let me stand in the way of any jewelry purchases). I love that you never really know who will send you a valentine—the boy you dated in college, your eighty-year-old father, or your five-year-old piano student. Little surprises are my favorite.

I can't tell you how disgusted I feel when I hear a man say he can't think of anything to do for his one, true love on Valentine's Day. Baloney. Can't be bothered is more like it. I can think of dozens of things ANYONE can do. For example, if you want to steer around crowded restaurants filled with smooching couples, or you wisely wish to avoid another charge on your credit card, pick up an inexpensive bottle of wine and a take-away appetizer on your way home from work. I think there is something particularly festive about Chinese food, something to do with the boxes, maybe, but it could also be the chopsticks or the fortune cookies. However, since I won't be there, get whatever works for the two of you. Set the stage for a romantic picnic in your home—NOT the kitchen table or anywhere else you normally eat. Spread a tablecloth or blanket on the floor. Avoid the kids' sheets with Disney characters splashed across them. Buzz Lightyear is not going to set the mood you are looking for. Light a candle. (Men: Look in the drawer with the flashlight, batteries, and matches. Find the candles without asking your wife where she keeps them, which is a real buzz-kill.) Use a piece of your wedding china to plate the appetizer and two crystal goblets. (They're in the china cabinet in the dining room, not in the kitchen with the coffee mugs.) Blindfold your wife. Lead her to your romantic nook. She'll be impressed. I promise. Total financial outlay: less than twenty bucks if you don't get carried away in the wine store.

You could also ask your wife to meet you for lunch at a favorite spot or somewhere new and exotic. Stop along the way to buy flowers from a street vendor like you are a character in a romantic comedy. Fill up her arms with blossoms. Every time you hand her a flower, pay her a compliment to go with it. You might say, "Lilies—the first flowers I ever sent you," or "Red roses—remember the ones on our honeymoon?" A girl can get drunk on compliments. If you can't think of any compliments, make some up. This is a good time to use your imagination for something more than the possibilities for the final-four bracket in college basketball.

If you are on a tight budget, stop by the public library and check out your wife's favorite romantic movie. Watch it with her. Pretend that you love it, too. You could also write a poem for your wife. WAIT! COME BACK! It doesn't have to be original. You can check out a volume of poetry at the same library where you check out videos. (Yes, your library card can actually be used for books as well as movies.) A little too uptown for your taste? Think about song lyrics if that makes it easier for you. I never met a man in my life who didn't think he could write a great song. It doesn't have to rhyme. You could write a haiku, short and sweet. Heck, you could write a funny limerick. Give yourself extra points for dirty words. It is Valentine's Day, after all. Lighten up. Have some fun with it. Write your poem on a paper heart you cut out yourself. Sign it. Put it in an envelope with your valentine's name on it. I guarantee you that points will be awarded for effort.

I especially love that Valentine's Day is the one day in the entire year when everybody else seems inclined to eat as much chocolate as I do on a regular basis. This holiday is a guilt-free, chocolate-eating-free-for-all, and that is absolution bound to make me sweetly disposed toward others. If you can afford it, go for elaborately wrapped, expensive chocolate, but remember that you can get the same result if you go to the drugstore and load up a bag with every candy bar your wife enjoys most. Show you've been paying attention to her candy preferences over the years, and she will remember why she fell in love with you. For example, if you know your wife is partial to Almond Joy candy bars even though she hates almonds, have a bag of Almond Joys all ready for her with the almonds already sucked off. She will know that you are, indeed, her soul mate.

Homemade valentine cards are the best thing about Valentine's Day. (I've written about this before in a chapter called "The Pity-Party Box" in my first book. If you have not read that—or my second book—you need to get on that. I can't keep catching you up.) I keep the valentines my children made for me when they were preschoolers in a box under my bed, and when I get the urge to have DNA tests performed on them to see if they are, indeed, the same children I gave birth to years ago, the squiggly writing and shakily drawn hearts remind me of the years when my children thought I was the most extraordinary human on the planet. Now, of course, they look at me like I have three heads, leprosy, or like a guest who accidentally burps in the middle of a wedding.

Best of all, I love that on Valentine's Day, my husband always gives me a romantic card that makes me feel loved—even if I was cheerfully thinking of divorcing him a scant twenty-four hours before. My husband has never failed to acknowledge Valentine's Day. That might be the reason we've been married for so many of them. Sometimes we were broke on Valentine's Day, sometimes not. It never mattered. As I tell my sons, a single flower or one beautifully wrapped chocolate says the same thing as a dozen.

Even the history of St. Valentine is romantic. Theological scholars don't know that much about him, but I like the theory that he helped persecuted Christians wed in secret. Maybe if he had done a little matchmaking for the emperor, he could have kept his head. Of course, then he wouldn't have been a saint. The suffering and traumatic denouement are requirements for sainthood. My children will tell you that I have a "thing" for saints. If you don't know your saints, I urge you to do some reading in this area. Saints' lives are colorful, to say the least. You don't make it to sainthood by living a boring life. Passion. Dedication. Romance. The saints have all that in spades. Little warning: it never ends well.

Go ahead. Roll your eyes. There's nothing you can say about Valentine's Day that will make me change my mind. Of course, I realize it's a made-up holiday. I know it's a rainmaker for florists and greeting-card vendors. The thing is: I don't care. I understand that many people see Valentine's Day as the cliché of all clichés. I just don't think the cliché is anything to be ashamed of.

I promise you that a construction-paper valentine, cut out with the kitchen scissors, with a romantic sentiment scrawled across it in a man's own handwriting, is one of the most romantic gestures I know. Even now, a homemade valentine makes me wish I carried cloth hankies in my handbag every day rather than just to funerals. I hate having to wipe away sentimental tears with paper napkins that say Pizza Hut on them. It cheapens the moment.

The thing about clichés is that they get to be clichés by appealing to a large demographic. I'm not one bit embarrassed about being a member of the Valentine's Day fan club. I say we women should stop apologizing for having a soft spot for this holiday. While I'm confessing, let me just go ahead and say that I also love bubble baths, milk chocolate, the occasional trashy novel, and shopping for fun (see chapter four, "A Shopping Philosophy"). Is that so wrong? Why are simple pleasures the subject of such ridicule? I don't understand that at all. Pure snobbery, I think.

Every woman in the world, from age twelve or so until senility, is looking for romance, yearning for it, actually, in everyday life. Sadly, it is very rare. It takes so little effort, time, or money, really, for men to be romantic. Sure, Valentine's Day puts the pressure on publicly, but we all know a few men out there who need a jumpstart, men who say, "What? Is it Valentine's Day already? Didn't I just buy you a Christmas present?" A man who says things like that is not, I repeat *not*, what we are looking for in any way, shape, or form.

What we want is the Cinderella ending. It's a long shot. Real life interrupts good intentions, lifelong promises, and heartfelt pledges of eternal love. Every grown-up woman knows that. To all you men out there, I say: If you've never made a big romantic gesture in your life, this is the one day of the year when it would not seem corny. On February 14, every woman you know—old, young, fat, skinny, married, single, divorced, sweet, or mean as a cottonmouth—EVERY woman checks the mail carefully for a valentine with her name on the envelope. She answers the door with a fast-beating heart, hoping for a blossom or two, and she checks under her pillow, on the kitchen table, in her car, and in your coat pocket to see if there is a small surprise there for her from you.

The Big V

I was born on Valentine's Day. The real problem I have with the holiday that happens to fall on my birthday is that it leads men to believe, quite wrongly, that women want romance on a yearly basis. They do not. They want romance all the time. (Ref: "One Romantic Gesture," paragraph five, by Melinda. I rest my case. I'm sure her husband, the judge, will rule in my favor on this one.) Men who think that singing, cutting up construction paper into hearts, making fancy dinner reservations, saying mushy stuff on Valentine's Day, et al, will somehow give them credit for the next 365 days are sorely mistaken. They will get a romance credit that lasts until February 15.

Because people born on Valentine's Day are expected to be at least somewhat romantic, throughout my life I've collected little bits of wisdom and information about the holiday, which in the spirit of goodwill and romance, I will share with you now.

The inspiration for Valentine's Day, or more properly, St. Valentine's Day, was a first-century martyr named St. Valentine, who was buried near Rome on February 14. Aside from being difficult to spell, *martyr* means, "one who gets whacked for no good reason." *Valentine* itself is derived from the Latin *valens*, which means, roughly translated, *worthy*.

I believe our modern culture has confused *traumatic* with *romantic*. Personally, I don't consider getting beat upside the head a particularly loving gesture. I try to avoid death and martyrdom whenever possible.

The symbolism associated with Valentine's Day is likewise dubious. It's the only holiday whose chief symbol, namely Cupid, is armed. He carries around a bow and arrow and shoots people in the backside.

Take the other holiday figures, for example: Do you see Santa Claus with a sawed-off shotgun? "Ho, Ho, Ho! Put your hands in the air!" Do Leprechauns wield bazookas? "Make my day, laddie!" Are the Easter Bunny, Uncle Sam, and the Tooth Fairy part of a militia that trains in the backwoods of Mississippi?

Well, maybe.

But at least other holiday characters give you stuff: pots of gold, presents, cash, eggs, and W-2 forms. And if Santa is a touch overweight, he hides it well by not running around in Speedos with a band of cherubim.

That's right. Cupid is nude. Nekkid. And worse, he's fat. Couldn't the greeting-card people have picked a Greek god that was attractive, say, Venus or Adonis? Why pick Jack Black in a thong?

The first paper valentine was written sometime in the 1400s. Five hundred years later, I scribbled my first valentine as a kindergartner. It took three horses worth of glue trying to get all my glitter and those little lacy things to stay on the red construction paper.

When my sweetie, Ginger Airhart (a six-year-old bombshell), got the card, I'm fairly sure it was the poetic "Love, Morgan" inscription that won her over—of course, the noxious glue fumes probably helped.

Over the years, Bugs Bunny, Daffy Duck, and even the Partridge family graced my little love notes. What I liked about those valentines is that they were neutral. "What's up Doc?" or

"Have a Loony Tunes Valentine's!" didn't necessarily mean you were out sitting in some tree with that person. As a result, everyone got valentines, including Billy Cooper, who ate boogers and wore headgear that was big enough to pick up Radio Free Europe.

But then in junior high school, the meaning of Valentine's Day changed. Only the brave and adventurous gave cards to the opposite sex. I tried that once.

Suzanna St. John, one of the prettier creatures in the eighth grade, was my biology lab partner, which meant we got to do romantic things together like cut up frogs and baby pigs. On that fateful Valentine's Day, I wrote her an anonymous love poem and strategically placed it atop her vivisected rat kidney. Then I waited for what seemed like an eternity for her to come into the classroom.

When at last she appeared and found the poem, I casually pretended to be inspecting a giant earthworm while my little biology-beloved read my sonnet. Finally, she looked up at me and said, after a dramatic pause, "Did you write this?"

"Uh, ah, well, um, er . . . yes," I bravely said. I was fighting to hold down the PB&J I'd eaten for lunch.

"Who is it about?" As you can see, Suzanna was (and still is) a get-to-the-point kind of girl.

If I'd been a suave sort of guy, I would have calmly said, "You," and shot her a steely gaze with the baby blues. But under the mighty power of an eighth-grade woman's question, I admit, I caved and blurted the first woman who came to mind, "The Statue of Liberty."

Okay, so maybe Lady Liberty wasn't the best of answers. I tried to show Suzanna that the poem really was about our nation's leading landmark. I remember changing one line to, "Your skin is like a crumpled, green, one-dollar bill."

She smiled, carefully folded the poem, and placed it in her purse, and we got on with obliterating various barnyard animals.

But in my heart, I'd like to think she didn't believe me.

In college, I was told by a female friend (in strictest and

utmost confidence), that *Miss Birmingham-Southern* wanted me to ask her out. Today, that seems quaint. The modern method is to simply send your crush a text message or look up their profile on Facebook. The friend subterfuge is less important. But I digress.

"Miss BSC is so tired of boring boys," my friend told me, "so be creative."

I wracked my brain trying to be creative. Sonnets! Poems! A singing telegram on Valentine's! But I was a broke college kid and couldn't afford a telegram. Rhyming verse has never been my strong point, either. My mom was an opera singer, so I can carry a tune . . . thus I decided to send her a singing telegram without getting Western Union involved. Stop.

Gina, the lovely *Miss Birmingham-Southern*, worked part-time at Victoria's Secret. So I decided to woo her with a serenade at Victoria's Not-So-Secret Secret to ask her out. Naturally, I ran this by my friend Simone, who wholeheartedly agreed that my idea was creative. Simone also vowed to keep it an absolute secret from her friend, *Miss Birmingham-Southern*. In the hindsight afforded by the many schemes and machinations I have heard my wife go through in order to set up a friend on a date, anything approaching "secrecy" between two girlfriends, when it comes to the subject of dating and dates, seems highly implausible.

To this day, I still blush walking through the lingerie section of Sears on the way to the power tools, so how I ever managed to sing "It Had to be You" in the midst of a bunch of panties and brassieres at Victoria's Secret, I'll never know. But sing I did—I crooned in the pantaloons, sang an F-sharp in the double-D section, and when it was over, the whole store, including just about every sister from *Miss Birmingham-Southern's* sorority who just *happened* to be shopping there that evening, broke into applause. The date didn't work out so hot, but no matter; I'd been romantic. It also helped me get over my fear of asking a girl out. Once you sing to someone, in an unmentionable store, in front of every coed at your college, well, calling a pretty girl on the phone doesn't seem that scary.

Well, actually, that's not true. It was still scary. My problem was that I could get a little tongue-tied sometimes. Like the Valentine's Day I first asked out Mrs. Murphy. You see, I'd been trying to ask her out, in person, for months. Yet she was always busy. So I finally decided to ask her out on the phone. I rang and rang and re-rang her home line, trying to catch her (imagine my mortification, years later, when I found out that she'd had one of the first Caller ID boxes in New York). Impatient, I decided to ask her out on her answering machine.

However, this presented a dilemma. I couldn't just make up what I was going to say on the fly. I'm a writer! So I carefully wrote out a very clever message, then rehearsed it a few times to sound natural, and took the plunge. It all went very well until the last line, which read, "Give me a call when you have a chance." Unfortunately, I said, "Give me a *chance* when you have a call. Or a minute. Or, oh damn."

Mrs. Murphy still has that message—my voice-mail equivalent of a bouquet of roses or a box of chocolates. My gaffe, I suppose, showed the true meaning of Valentine's Day—that I was vulnerable, worthy, and had a little heart . . . *valens* of her affection.

PART II

You Say, "Tomato"; I Say, "Where's the Lettuce and the Bacon?"

Chapter 10

Romancing the South

One Romantic Gesture

Melinda Rainey Thompson

There comes a time in every woman's life when she realizes that she can't remember her last romantic moment. It might have been weeks, months, or even years ago. This can happen even when she's a happily married person who wouldn't change a thing about her life. It can also happen when her significant other has moved on—as in six feet under or just off to plow new fields, so to speak. No woman plans to wake up one morning thinking: when was the last time someone kissed me like I was the most important woman in the world? It's easy to fall into relationship ruts, the habitual hello/goodbye peck on the lips. It isn't that we never get those romantic moments anymore, but after twenty or more years, they don't come around that often. This makes me sad.

Sometimes, I think about the little old ladies I see at church whose husbands have been dead for years. One of the things I like best about my church, the Episcopal Church, is that there is a moment during every service when the priest says, "May the peace of the Lord be always with you." The appropriate response is always, "And also with you," just in case you didn't know. We Episcopalians do a lot of talking back in our church. You can see how I fit right in. This is the moment in every service when people to your right and left, people in front of you and behind you, and sometimes people several pews away take the time to greet you, shake your hand, give you a hug, pat you on the back, or lift you off your feet with bear-hug enthusiasm. There's something life affirming about seeing a room full of people all reaching out to one another—friends and strangers alike.

I especially enjoy the wide-eyed look of a guest, unfamiliar with this custom, who gets ambushed in the middle of a peace-loving pew. Guests tend to tense up a little at first, as if they're not quite sure what to expect from these constantly shifting (literally, not theologically, Lord knows) Christians. Every pew is in constant motion—sit, stand, kneel, stand, kneel—and there's quite a bit of room for personal choice, so no two rows of congregants look alike. I can understand a stranger's wariness. Christianity, like all religions, has a checkered past. Naturally, I make sure to greet strangers first, just so they know the natives are friendly.

A few Sundays ago, an older parishioner told me, as we were exiting the pew at the end of the service, that she looks forward to the exchange of peace because it is often the only time she is touched by another human being all week. That confession, a comment tossed carelessly to me over her shoulder, brought me to my knees. I sat in the church for a long time after the service thinking about it.

Since then, I've been thinking more and more about the loss of small, thoughtful, romantic gestures in our daily lives. Every year, they seem to get fewer and farther between. Nobody takes the time anymore. When did you last receive a letter with no agenda, just to say hello, share thoughts, and catch up with news? I think I get two or three letters like that a year. Somehow, we've reduced the definition of all romantic gestures to exchanges between spouses, boyfriends, and girlfriends. That is far too narrow a view, in my opinion. We need to look back a few centuries to remind ourselves of courtly manners, of chivalrous behavior, and small tokens of love and friendship within a community of people committed to the welfare of one another.

Don't panic. I'm not about to light incense, meditate, or proselytize here. The loss I'm mourning here has to do with neighborly kindness. The age-old question of the lawyer to Jesus, "Who, then, is my neighbor?" troubles me. Before you begin to hum "We Are the World" or "Kumbaya," or you succumb to the urge to shrug your shoulders or gag, let me explain. We need to revive the custom of small, romantic gestures in our daily lives. It's the only thing I can think of to beat the terrible monotony of the daily grind. We need to perform a daily act of kindness. I don't care if it's a cliché. It's a cliché because it's true. (Yes, yes, I know this topic is a little cloying, but I'll get back to being sassy and sarcastic in a minute. Don't worry. I can't do "sweet" for long. It goes against my natural inclinations.)

My premise here is that romantic moments are possible even among non-romantic partners. Think about a teenage boy helping an old lady unload the groceries from her car. Watch as a stranger helps a young mother struggling to get a stroller through an airport security checkpoint. Last week, I witnessed a spontaneous round of "Happy Birthday" and an accompanying cheer for a woman on her ninety-fifth birthday. What are the odds there will be a ninety-sixth? The opportunities for romantic moments are everywhere.

The most romantic thing that happened to me this week involved the return of some Tupperware. Okay, I admit that it sounds fairly prosaic, but I lead a very ordinary life. I don't get out that much, and I'm telling you that I got that melt-my-heart moment with the return of some cheap, plastic storage containers.

Here's the story. A friend of mine, Roy, had shoulder surgery. I know, I know. You wouldn't think someone named Roy could be romantic, but he is. It's Roy's wife you call if you want the score for the football game, but it's Roy who gave his wife stained-glass church windows for her twenty-first birthday, windows that they still have in their house today, four children and many years later. Obviously, in my opinion, Roy is an example of a Southern man who has been "raised right."

I made dinner for his family because that's what we do

in the South. It doesn't really matter what is wrong with you; we send food, no matter what. You aren't required to actually eat it. That's not really the point. We just have to cook it and deliver it. It's part of the social contract down here. Get it? It's a romantic gesture. I delivered his dinner (roast, mashed potatoes, lima beans, tiny bridge biscuits, and homemade pound cake with fresh peach sauce, in case you're wondering) in cheap, throw-away plastic because it is mean to deliver food to people in need of it and then leave them with a job to do—to return your dishes. On my way out of his house, I bragged on his gardenia bushes, which are taller than I am.

Imagine my surprise when I returned home the next day after a round of high school baseball with my son (I wonder what other people do in June?) to find all my disposable containers artistically arranged on my porch, with a handwritten thank-you note propped next to them and—here's the clincher—a gardenia nosegay on top. I tell you that those gardenias just about did me in, and I pride myself on being decidedly unsentimental. I am NEVER a crybaby.

I've reached a point in my life where I am not often surprised, but those gardenias surprised me. It was such a lovely touch of civility in an otherwise hot, sweaty day. Roy's gardenias were a romantic gesture that made me happy deep down, all the way to my toes. First of all, it just happened to be my anniversary, and my husband was campaigning out of town. I was a little blue already. (For those of you who have not read my earlier books—which, of course, I urge you to do immediately—my husband is a judge. He has been forced to endure taunts on the campaign trail about a chapter he inspired in one of my books, "Sleeping with a Snoring Man." The poor man cringes every time I start a new book. I remind him that you can't worry about everything. Who knows what is going to happen? We could get run over by a forklift at Lowe's tomorrow when we go to buy fertilizer. I think he secretly fears I will be struck down by a vengeful bolt of lightning. Perhaps that explains why he doesn't stand too close to me in public.)

Back to my present story: There were definitely no gardenias coming from my husband's direction. Also, I hate hot weather, so, naturally, after sitting through a blistering baseball doubleheader, I was a little on the teary side already.

As I stood on my front porch contemplating my Tupperware and gardenia bouquet, my mind flashed back to my wedding day, twenty-one years ago—almost to the minute. More than anything, I wanted a wedding bouquet made out of gardenias. "No way," the overbearing florist told my mother and me. "They bruise too easily. They'll never make it." Of course, what she really meant was, "No way am I making that kind of effort. I'm making your bouquet up hours before the wedding. Pick roses like everybody else, and be done with it. That will be much easier for me." I'd have been happy with gardenias cut from someone's yard, wrapped with green floral tape, and tied with white satin ribbon.

Gardenias are my favorite flower on earth. Nothing is so fragrant and lush, so essentially Southern in my mind (although I am exceedingly partial to paperwhites, too). I can remember taking naps as a child with the windows open and the scent of gardenias in full bloom blowing through the house. I swear that I can still close my eyes and smell them. Recently, I finally paid for some much-needed landscaping of my old foliage, and I added a bed of gardenias, which bloomed out so fragrant I was looking for reasons to open and close my front door. Sadly, they are a different species from the traditional blossoms I wanted. They have only one layer of petals like a daisy. I've never seen this species before, so I was really disappointed. In a previous gardenia quest, I planted gardenias only to find out they were dwarf plants with blooms that would only be big enough for Barbie's wedding bouquet. I seem destined for gardenia disasters.

This week, I got my romantic moment. I was reminded that just when you think your life will never offer up another romantic moment, it could happen. One sweet gesture can turn an ordinary day into a special one, and, on my anniversary, I was reminded of one of the reasons I love being a Southern woman. I really, really do love Southern men.

How to Romance a Southern Woman

Hold her hand voluntarily in public without
looking embarrassed about it.

If you really want to go for broke, turn her hand over and
press a kiss on her palm. She'll swoon in your arms.
I guarantee it.

Ask her if she'd like you to beat somebody up for her. Don't
worry. She won't actually ask you to do it. It would just be
nice if someone would occasionally offer.

Just once, instead of the usual perfunctory peck on the lips
before you leave town for a few days, grab that woman by the
waist, pull her up against you, and plant a kiss on her lips
she'll remember to her dying day.

Start her car one cold morning so that it is unexpectedly
toasty when she climbs in for the first foray of the day. Leave
a note on the windshield—not a Post-it reminding her to buy
milk—a LOVE letter. It doesn't have to be a Shakespearean
sonnet. A hand-drawn heart and your initials can reduce even
the meanest matron to a weepy puddle of sloppy sentiment.

While she finishes cleaning up the kitchen, run a bubble bath
for her. Light candles. Put a magazine or a trashy book
by the tub for her to read. Lead her there with

her eyes closed before the water cools. Smile at her. Kiss her on the lips. Then leave her alone to enjoy it.

Bring her a guilty pleasure for no reason at all: a banana split, petit fours, cheese straws, milk chocolate, or whatever you know really pots her plant. If she doesn't like those things, bring them to me. I do.

Take her on a date. PRETEND. The date cannot involve work clients, church functions, children's activities, or any other mundane life events. CHOOSE to spend time with her. Woo her. You're older now. You should be better at it. She might surprise you and woo you right back.

Before she falls asleep one night, tell her about your favorite memory of her—extra points for details. Caution: make sure you get the details right. If your favorite memory of her turns out to actually involve a former wife/girlfriend, things could get ugly.

Make a sacrifice for her—of time, money, patience, or real blood. Women are biologically programmed to fall for strong providers and protectors. Use basic biology to your advantage. Real men are willing to take a bullet for the women they love, and nothing is more attractive to a woman than a wounded warrior.

Romance for Less

When I first met my wife, *broke* only begins to describe the depths of my pennilessness. My first big magazine job at *Vanity Fair* paid twelve thousand dollars a year. My rent in New York City totaled twelve thousand dollars per annum. You do the math. We joked that the magazine was a nice place to work if your parents could afford to send you there. I refused to ask anyone for a nickel, and as a result of a crackers-and-peanut-butter diet, I dropped down to one hundred fifty pounds. I am six foot two, so one hundred fifty pounds flattered me not. I resembled an emaciated Ichabod Crane. (If you're looking to shed a few pounds, try starting a new career as a magazine writer.)

It was here, at the nadir of my financial life, that I met the sophisticated and charming future Mrs. Murphy. Ahh, cruel fate. Just going to a movie in New York City cost more than my first car. Cab fare: $40. Movie: $20. Popcorn: $876.

Add to that tally the fact that I'm from the South. It never occurred to me that I could just show up to a date empty-handed. Good Lord, no. Southern women expect certain gestures, and out of ignorance or sentimentality, I expected that

Yankee women would expect those gestures as well. Especially pretty Yankee women.

Romantic gesture #1: flowers.

Romantic gesture #2: chocolates.

And in my family, we have romantic gesture #3: a book. Yes, a book. My great-grandmother broke ground by being one of the first six women to attend the University of Alabama. Gentlemen callers who asked Great-Grandmama on a date were expected to arrive with flowers, chocolate . . . and a book. Later in life, she'd swoop her arm across the vast expanse of books in her library and boast, "Not only was I the best-read girl at the University, I was also the prettiest."

Never mind she only had five competitors among five thousand fellows.

Books proved to be my salvation in my courtship with Mrs. Murphy. Every publisher in America sent *Vanity Fair* a stack of books, hoping the magazine might tout a few in its pages. The vast majority of these books ended up discarded on a lonely table next to the service elevator, fondly referred to as the "freebie table" by starving interns and assistants. If untouched, the contents of said table were thrown away every Friday night.

Being the entrepreneurial type, I grabbed two bags and filled them with books on Friday evenings before my big dates with Mrs. Murphy. Two bags held approximately fifty pounds of discarded *libres*. I then walked from the *Vanity Fair* offices on 45th Street and Madison Avenue to 12th Street and Broadway, a distance of 1.6 miles of honking cabs, delivery boys on bicycles, lost tourists, and ten thousand stoplights. By the time I made it to my destination, the Strand Bookstore, my fingers clutched the handles of the bags with gnarled and bloodless tendons.

The dusty fellows in the basement of the Strand would glance through the pile of books, looking for something interesting and sellable. I became imaginary friends with popular writers. Tom Wolfe was always good for $5. Willie Morris might fetch $2.50. Stephen King commanded $6. That's how I knew he was big time. The rest got heaped onto a scale, weighed, and I received a dollar per pound. A good Friday book haul netted $60.

I thus became quite adept at bargain-basement romance. My first date with the future Mrs. Murphy consisted of a trip to the Metropolitan Museum of Art, which had a suggested donation of $20. Note the word *suggested*. (Whenever I visit the museum today, I am racked with guilt and toss some extra dough in the pot because I took *suggested* to mean about $2.) Drinks atop of the museum overlooking the park usually cost an additional $20. Dinner was $50. Like Congress, I ran substantial deficits while dating Mrs. Murphy.

After our first date, I wanted to deliver flowers in the grand tradition of my Southern upbringing. The price for flower delivery in New York ranges somewhere between $50 and a corporate Gulfstream jet. Luckily, someone in my apartment building threw out a decent old vase, none the worse for its former floral contents. A piece of leftover ribbon, $10 worth of roses from the local Korean deli, and a three-mile walk was all it took to deliver my romantic gesture.

Have you ever tried walking any distance with a glass jar brimming with a gallon of water, sloshing on hapless pedestrians and small dogs? Love hurts, particularly in the forearms. On our date, Mrs. Murphy had mentioned that her family called her "Glamour-puss" for her penchant for getting dressed up. I'd just seen *All About Eve* for the first time and remembered that Bette Davis said, "Now don't go falling for some New York glamour-puss." So that's what I wrote on the card.

I didn't hear from my beloved for three days and had begun to panic when her response arrived in the mail: "Hold on: it's going to be a wild and bumpy ride." (That, of course, is the moment I knew I was going to marry her—she played along.)

Our flat-broke courtship continued for two years: free concerts in the park, window-shopping, picnics, church services, and cocktail receptions for various corporations. It is amazing the places you can crash in a threadbare blue blazer.

Now, ten years later, marriage and promotions have reaped

greater prosperity. Velveeta no longer shimmers with such a luxurious sheen. Mrs. Murphy and I think nothing of a trip to a movie, though I still resent paying the cost of a new Buick for a bucket of popped corn. I order dinner without looking at the price tag. I no longer sneak into corporate luncheons and talk to people named Bob about actuarial tables in exchange for crudités.

Likewise, my romantic gestures cost more these days. I buy real flowers from a real florist. I purchase real scarves from a store with a fancy bag. I choose perfume that must be squeezed out of rare topiary arrangements by French virgins on the first equinox of spring. Problem is, holidays creep up on married men. Christmas. Valentine's Day. Anniversary. Birthday. I'm forgetting one, probably. Then damn, the holiday, anniversary, birthday, whatever, becomes this week, today, now, this second. I, caught unawares, sit at my desk mumbling, "Romantic! Must be romantic!"

Where am I going to get a used vase and some ribbon? Shoot, what insurance function can we crash tonight? Maybe she'd like crackers, cheap wine, and a loaf of cheese substance? I usually resort to the old reliables: perfume, flowers, a trinket from a nice jeweler. Every man should memorize his jeweler's number.

Mrs. Murphy, always gracious, feigns surprise upon opening the virginal French perfume or pair of earrings. Still, I know in my heart she wants romance. Romance not dictated by a holiday calendar. Romance that takes spontaneity: it takes thoughtfulness; it doesn't cost much. You can't buy an afternoon in a sunlit park or an evening gazing at majestic works of art in a museum gallery. You can't purchase animated conversation and a quickened pulse. Mrs. Murphy wants—no, deserves—romance for no reason, romance just because she chose me.

A trio of soft white roses opened into full bloom in my garden not long ago. I've transplanted, tended, pruned, sprayed, and fretted over them for three years. Finally, the buds of my work blossomed. I could hear Mrs. Murphy upstairs and busy, so I eased outside, cut the roses, and placed them in an old Mason jar tied with some twine from my toolshed.

I left them on the kitchen counter with a note that said, "Glad I fell for that New York glamour-puss."

How to Romance Any Southern Male

Get nekkid

Chapter 11

Surviving Crash Diets

Diet Drama

Melinda Rainey Thompson

Here it is: the chapter I said I would never write. You'd think by this time in my life I'd have learned never to say *never*. Whenever I make that emphatic *never* statement, it seems like that is the very thing that God lines up for me to do next. I'm plenty disgusted with myself for sinking this low. I had every intention of writing a chapter about something important—like the electoral college or global warming. Unfortunately, this chapter about dieting keeps lighting up my brain like the "Hot Doughnuts Now" sign at Krispy Kreme. I know from past experience that the only way I'm going to get that light to go off is to go ahead and write about it. Writing is a little bit like being temporarily possessed by an evil spirit or the throw-up virus.

I'd rather talk about almost anything else—changes in the tax code, the infield fly rule in baseball, or why teenagers wear their hair so long that it interferes with their vision and their pants so low you can see their underwear. I'd rather pull up my shirt and compare and contrast caesarian-section scars than have another dieting discussion. We all know what we should do. It's just very hard to do.

Dieting is a subject where otherwise sane, logical human

beings lose their minds. I have heard women describe diets so bizarre you would swear they were designed by terrorists intent on bringing us capitalists to our knees. I know many people who are normal in every way—except for their religious devotion to strange diets they believe keep them thin.

For example, have you ever heard of the God Diet? You can eat anything you want on this diet as long as God made it—fruit, vegetables, meat, bread, whatever. You can't eat foods with preservatives, artificial sweeteners, dyes, or anything man-made. Also, you can't connect the dots in a tenuous legal argument, such as: God made man; man builds factories; factories bake delicious cookies; therefore, God makes Oreos, and I can eat them. Nope. That is cheating. I checked.

Another favorite diet is the Weekends-Off Plan. The title says it all. It is based on the premise that all foods are possible in moderation. If you eat moderately all week, it is logical to assume you can loosen up on the weekends. However, if you eat like the New Orleans Saints' starting lineup on the weekends, this may not be the diet for you.

The most common diet out there is probably the calorie-counting or fat-gram-counting method. This is the grand-mamma of all diets, the inspiration for all the big moneymakers. These dieters will drive you nuts. Not only will they count the calories in everything they eat, but they'll count the calories in everything you eat, too. An endless tally will be updated throughout the day. If one of these devotees is involved in a car accident, you might hear, "How many calories are in this IV bag? This could throw off my count for the whole day!"

The most unusual diet I ever heard of is the Jell-O Diet. Some people love Jell-O because it satisfies a craving for sweets without sacrificing many calories. Jell-O's consistency turns me off. The way it suspends fruit in a transparent, semi-solid liquid strikes me as unnatural. For those of you who are not freaked out by Jell-O, the rule for this diet is that you can eat anything you want—as long as it is suspended in Jell-O. I have a friend who tossed a medium-rare steak and a baked potato with all the fixings into a mold of lime Jell-O. She swears she ate the whole thing without throwing up. She said it wasn't that bad.

Bottom line on dieting: I don't care that much whether I'm fat or not. In addition, it doesn't bother me one bit if you are fat or not. To those of you who are about to bow up in heart-healthy indignation: zip it. I get it. I care that we don't die of heart attacks, strokes, diabetes, or cancer, of course I do, but that's not really where I'm going with this *humor* chapter, okay? I care that we eat healthy, in a half-hearted yet sincere way, but I don't care enough to be obsessive about it. There is a world of dieting difference in this distinction. Either you're with me here, or this would be a good time for you to skip on to the next chapter in the book. If you like to sample every single item on the buffet table like I do, keep reading.

I think my views on dieting reflect what ordinary people think. The media, on the other hand, love dieting extremes. Every new diet craze gets more television airtime than the death of a former president. I suspect a thin-person conspiracy. If you believe everything you see on television, you might think that all Americans are obsessed with losing weight and having sex all the time. You might also assume that Americans murder each other in bizarre and devious ways at the drop of a hat and are generally spoiled, materialistic, hateful, disloyal, fat, and abnormally concerned with having extremely white teeth.

Regular people laugh at diet gurus the same way they laugh at the tabloids' latest alien abduction stories. They may read the headlines when they are trapped in the grocery store checkout line, but they don't *believe* them. (I've read the vomit bag on an airplane when it was in my line of sight. So what?)

Most of us have dieting figured out. In the scheme of things that matter—child rearing, marriages, jobs, our communities, the state of the real world—how thin or fat you are isn't important. I find it amazing that I actually have to write that down in a book.

We've all made little deals with the devil. We find what we can live with. I order the garden salad for lunch with chocolate cake for dessert. This makes perfect sense to me. Other women scarf down a second helping of pasta and then burn it off with an extra mile on the treadmill. Sometimes, we just buy bigger underwear.

Here's the down-and-dirty truth: every diet works—for a while. Then, real life comes back to bite you on the fanny when it becomes increasingly unappetizing to pack your tofu-sprout sandwich for work and eat it across from someone chowing down on a cheeseburger from paradise. The truth is that in order to lose weight, you have to actually eat less, exercise, and refrain from lots of delicious, fatty, salty, calorie-laden, addictive, processed-food items which we actually enjoy eating as a fun activity all by itself. I defy anyone to tell me a more fun thing to do than to spend a morning working my way through a big bag of Reese's cups. If I could find a way to work lime-flavored vodka into that without being sick, I would lay claim to my Elysian fields. (You didn't think a woman who loves Reese's cups would make an Elysian Fields allusion; did you? You really shouldn't stereotype people.)

My husband is an experienced dieter. In the twenty-something years we have been married, I've lost count of the number of times he's lost fifty pounds or more. It's genetic. I'm convinced of it. We can eat the same thing for an entire weekend, and he gains weight in his face and chin like a chipmunk storing nuts for the winter. I never fully appreciated the suffering he went through trying to maintain his weight until I, too, had to lose a few pounds—ten pounds, to be exact. That's all I wanted to lose—not enough to change dress sizes or anything, just enough to make me feel less like a stuffed-sausage when wearing my favorite skirt. How hard could it be?

Plenty hard is what I found out. My husband can lose thirty or forty pounds in the time it takes me to lose ten pounds. Once I realized this, my nose was really out of joint. Weight loss is sexist? Who knew? This did not improve my temper one iota.

What I want, I told my husband in bed late one night, is to be my old thin self. *However*, I also want to eat whatever I want to eat whenever I want to eat it.

The man actually snorted out loud. "That's what everybody

wants, you idiot," he said, before turning off the light, rolling over, and going to sleep—while I was still in mid-discourse regarding the fascinating trials of my current ten-pound-weight-loss-campaign.

I spent a few minutes deciding whether or not to take offense. In the end, I decided I didn't have the energy to work up a good mad about his ill-mannered name-calling. The reality is that he was only telling the truth. We all want the same things—model-thin thighs and double-chocolate lattes with extra whipped cream. *C'est la vie.*

Suck It In

Hubber, blubber, boil, and flubber. The South has cooked its way into a mess by being ranked the number one region for obesity.

My advice? Eat more; worry less.

America is the fattest nation on earth. Thirty-three percent of us are overweight. And we've been pretty upset about it. But being worried about flab is part of the Great American Way. Where would Jane Fonda and Jenny Craig be without fat people? "Buns of Steel" and "Eight Minute Abs" might go broke. And what about all those skiing contraptions sold late at night on channel four that claim to make you slender? Thankfully, for the American economy, we buy all that stuff, shove it in the closet, and are still fat, just $899.99 poorer. Then there are those wealthier sad slobs who go to a medical doctor who has sold his twelve years of doctor school down the cellulite river by buying a supercharged Electrolux and charging people $1,000 a thigh to Roto-Root the fat cells out of their body.

So how do all those other nations stay alluringly thin while we Americans go to such trouble? Why are the British, Japanese, Germans, and Russians all so slim and trim? Well,

I've got the answer. All those other nations have thinner people because they eat less.

Fact is: it's easier for them to eat less because their food is disgusting. The British? Fish and chips—slimy fried eel from the polluted Thames River and soggy fries. The Japanese? Slimy eel and seaweed served raw. The Germans? Sour cabbage and crusty sausage. The Russians? Cabbage and potatoes.

Let's face it, if those countries had American institutions like all those snack cakes that sound like Vegas strip acts (Little Debbies, Ding Dongs, Ring Dings, Eskimo Pies, and Ho Hos), they'd blow up faster than Michael Moore at a Dairy Queen.

Okay, so there are some cultures that have good food and the people are thin. Take the nation of France, for instance. How do they stay thin? This is easy: they walk everywhere. Why? Because they don't have any decent Cadillacs and Buicks over there. If you drove a Peugeot, Renault, or Deux Cheveaux, you'd do most of your travel on foot, too. Walking is exercise, folks, and I'm firmly against it. I don't lift anything unless it falls on me or run anywhere unless I'm being chased.

Is it any wonder that, right here in the South, we've got more obese citizens than anywhere else on earth? What Yankee food can compare to grits and butter? Virginia ham? Chess pie? Fried chicken? Barbecue? Goobers and Co-Colas? MoonPies? Greasy cornbread? Bacon and fresh, juicy tomato sandwiches on white bread? Corn pudding? How 'bout pickled pigs' feet? Okay, perhaps there are some exceptions, but by and large, the South is a great place to chow down.

We have grub worth getting fat over. Gimmie a Po-boy and bowl of gumbo any day over some cabbage and a dead eel.

Now, that's not to say I'm not on a strict diet. I am, and it's one I've followed for years. I always make sure to eat the four Southern food groups at every meal: grease, salt, bourbon, and pie.

The very mention of these hallowed groups, which I call the *nutrition trapezoid*, may cause some poor, uneducated souls to recoil in horror. Pity them. Grease, salt, bourbon, and pie are the staples of my culinary roots. My mother could fry a dishrag and my father would eat it. And like it. A Southern-impaired guest once foolishly asked Mama why her fried chicken tasted so good. The answer lurks beneath her sink in an enormous coffee can full of bacon grease. By all outward appearances, we seem normal. To look at my thin, blonde mother, you would never suspect that she hoards bacon drippings with which to fry chicken, steak, ham, and just about anything else that will fit in her skillet. To her, lard is not a four-letter word. She's the only woman I know who can use an entire tub of Crisco in one cake (trust me; you'd love it). Using grease in our cooking is a Southern tradition we come by naturally, one that is as old as the South itself.

So it was with some alarm that I brought my New York sweetie to South Alabama to meet my folks when we were first courting. New Yorkers, by some weird twist of culinary evolution, never developed a taste for fried food. After seven years amongst them, I found the average New Yorker knows the meaning of tiramisu and cavatelli, but would sooner eat raw eel than consume a Southern staple like fried okra. "What the *\$#@ is an okra?" was a common refrain when I relayed this fact to Manhattanites.

Eager to impress my sweetheart on her first visit south, my grandfather decided to take us to the nicest restaurant in Red Level, Alabama—Green's Barbecue. My future bride, equally eager to impress my family, had worn her finest Chanel suit and was resplendently decked in a very tasteful strand of pearls. If you've ever set foot in a Deep South barbecue joint, I need not tell you that she looked ridiculous at Green's.

Mrs. Green came immediately to our table bearing menus (like I said, my family stands in high repute in the world of grease). Granddad waved those away and bellowed in the broad tenor of his ninety-three years, "I'll order for the girl! She'll have fried chicken, French fries, fried dill pickles, sweet tea, and some fried apple pie." After a moment he added, "with ice cream."

When the food arrived, I could see the future Mrs. Murphy mentally calculate how many billion fat grams were contained in the heaping mass of brown food before her. As I was contemplating whether this was the time to share with her that Mrs. Green's sweet tea had enough sugar in it to give a moose diabetes, she fiercely whispered to me through gritted teeth, "What the devil are those?" pointing to the basket of fried pickles.

"Just eat them or everyone will think you're a Yankee," I whispered back.

"I am a Yankee!" she said, losing her New York cool.

Shortly thereafter, I got wrapped up in a conversation with Uncle Mark about the Red Level Yacht Club, an organization he founded, but one that, curiously, has no yachts unless you count fancy bass boats. When I turned back to Amy to check her progress, she smiled sheepishly. The basket of pickles was empty. Only minute batter crumbles remained on the wax paper and her lapels. She'd inhaled those suckers like a Hoover on high.

Now, years later, a peek under our stove will reveal my bride's Southern conversion—a telltale tub of grease waits for the next course.

Worth Gaining a Few

Sweet tea

Real "Co-Colas" in the eight-ounce glass bottle

Biscuits. With sausage. Okay, and eggs. Alright, and maybe some butter and gravy.

Pecan pie

Chess pie

Banana cream pie

Lemon pie

Grits: with butter, cheese, bacon, and bacon

Fried chicken

Fried okra

Fried porkchops

Fried *anything*

Chapter 12

Vanity Unfair

Brace Yourself

Grown-up women and braces are not a good combination. There are worse combinations, of course, like grown-up women and tube tops or little old ladies with butterflies tattooed across their sagging granny bosoms. Some things are best experienced as a youthful rite of passage. Getting the school cafeteria's mystery meat stuck in your braces is an after-school television special for seventh graders. A middle-aged woman with spinach quiche stuck in her braces isn't nearly as endearing.

One of the last things you want to hear as a grown-up is that you need braces. It's like being told you have adult acne. Once my orthodontist told me that my teeth might fall out when I get old unless I do something about it now, it's hard to really forget that. I'm a rule follower. Nevertheless, I can't get over the feeling that braces are like Facebook profiles. Everyone seems to have them.

In America, orthodontists have stumbled upon a good thing, and they know it. They see women like me and know they can build a boathouse, plan a trip around the world, or pay for a semester of private-college tuition by correcting our imperfections. There's a whole world of moneymaking potential in a group of aging women who are vain enough and rich enough to pay for just about anything. I don't quite fit the mold. First of all, I'm not rich. Plus, I do not believe that one has to suffer to be beautiful, and I'm cheap. When vanity meets cheapness in my life, cheapness wins.

In many ways, orthodontists are like missionaries out to convert the natives in their zeal to enhance the smile of every adult with a bank account and a cross bite. You can just imagine how pleased I was to be referred to an orthodontist for a consultation. Nothing, and I mean nothing, prepares you for the sticker shock. Of course, your orthodontist won't even mention money. Physicians are above all that monetary unpleasantness. They merely offer you their best medical advice and then leave you alone in a room to come to terms with the new stinking lay of the land before sending in the office manager to divide your huge bill into monthly payments second only to your mortgage. A pretty smile is worth a million dollars—literally. I was tempted to ask what kind of smile I could get for around five hundred.

On the plus side, I was left to rail against genetic injustice in a room with a massage chair since my orthodontist's office is big-city plush. The parts of my anatomy that were in direct contact with the chair were happy to ante up any sum of money in order to return to the full-body massage once a month. Those chairs are a fabulously sneaky improvement on the old-fashioned dentist's chair. Orthodontists are tricky.

After the orthodontist broke the news, she introduced her hatchet lady (known in some circles as the office manager or bookkeeper). These people are slick. She knew just how to talk me down from the tree I was clinging to, and by the time I left her office, I felt like I was constitutionally entitled to those braces, and I really couldn't remember why I hadn't considered them before. I was convinced that my transformation from mousy, middle-aged woman to dynamic-smile-machine would make it all worth it. In the back of my mind, I thought it was entirely possible that Prince Charming had merely been waiting until my teeth were perfectly aligned to rescue me from suburbia.

Even the hatchet lady did not have the nerve to utter the grand total out loud. She wrote an obscene amount of money on a piece of paper, tucked it in a fancy folder to dress it up and cushion the blow, and slid the whole package across the table to me like a secret bid at an auction. That took guts. My first reaction was to laugh. "Is this in rubles?" I wanted to know. You could buy a kidney in some countries for the price of my braces. It's more than I paid for a semester of college. It's more than I have spent on my own personal entertainment in my whole life. I could buy tickets to about five hundred movies and order large sodas and popcorn for everyone in the joint with this kind of cash.

Of course, I won't be having popcorn for the next two years because popcorn is one of the many foods forbidden to those who wear braces. Naturally, I can't cheat because I have to set a good example for the teenagers in my house who also wear braces. Oh, yeah. We're paying for several sets of braces—*at the same time.* Clearly, if Mom cheats, then the whole social order as we know it will break down.

There are things no one wants to tell you about braces. That's mostly because they are so gross. You will be forever trying to dig out some piece of food from your braces. When you bite into a sandwich, you will look like an anaconda trying to swallow a monkey whole. Cutting up a cheeseburger into sixteen manageable bites is disgusting.

Also, braces hurt. They aren't "uncomfortable." They *hurt.* Vodka helps, but you can't drink all the time—can you? I am mortified to report that my tongue sometimes gets hung up in my braces. This is not a good look for me. I believe that I lose IQ points every time that happens. There is also a little thing called braces breath. Enough said, I think. Finally, although this isn't a well-documented complication, I have experienced braces claustrophobia. It takes massive self-control to resist grabbing a screwdriver and ripping these braces out of my mouth. I'm not sure hormonal women should be allowed anywhere near braces. Anything could happen. Without question, the worst part about braces is the price tag. It's like a two-year car payment. I am going to feel this pain for a long time.

Being told you need braces is not a popular diagnosis at any age, but it is much harder for adults to hear. Even the name, *braces*, sounds bad, doesn't it? It makes me think of iron lungs and birth defects. I know my teeth aren't perfect, but the American smile standard is as close to perfect as genes and human intervention can make it. The bar is very high—Olympic, really. You can recognize the flash of an American smile anywhere on earth. Is that good or bad? I can't decide. I'm pretty sure I want to get my braces in my American orthodontist's office, however, the one with the warm cookies and the massage chairs. You won't catch me standing in line in Romania for dental work. You only get one set of teeth. The next set comes in a box.

The question that haunts me is why in the world I would care about straightening my teeth at this stage of the game. I don't have big, scary buckteeth or anything like that. This is a lot like my logic in not losing that extra ten pounds I've been carrying around for a decade. Is my husband going to love me any less for the additional inch around my waist? I don't think so. He has a matching flotation device around his own waist.

My insurance company assures me that I don't need braces. It claims that braces are purely cosmetic work. The agent made it clear that the company has no intention of reimbursing me for a self-indulgent medical procedure. I got the impression that I should be ashamed for inquiring, as if my personal selfishness will prevent a bunch of orphan children from getting dental care. I bet you are just shocked to hear that, aren't you? My friendly insurance representative (who does not have any medical training, by the way) assured me that unless I get hit in the mouth with a baseball bat, I don't need orthodontic work. I considered, briefly, asking one of my baseball-playing boys to take a swing at me, but I found that, in the end, I am too big of a pansy to take one in the kisser for the family budget.

Without realizing it, I gave my orthodontist, a woman I absolutely adore, the opportunity she'd been looking for. She needed adult guinea pigs for a new kind of braces technology called iBraces. They go on the inside of your teeth, so they don't show. *Of course*, they cost more—a lot more. When I saw how much, I almost threw up. I have more money in this investment than my youngest child. In the end, I signed on the dotted line, and some robots (I'm not making this up) made braces for me, which were custom-tailored to my teeth. That seemed like a good idea. We Southern women love individual attention.

The first snag we ran into involved the molds that are used to make the braces. They have to be perfect. Preferably, Michelangelo himself should sculpt these things. It required three separate visits to my orthodontist to get them right. Finally, bossy woman that I am, I asked if I could do it myself. They filled up the trays. I stuck them in, and *voila!* (I was late for carpool; I didn't have any more time to fool around.) The orthodontist sent me home with a gift certificate to the hottest new clothing store in my neighborhood. I ended up with a red-and-black-polka-dot dress. I know it was hush money. Still, it was nice.

I plan to do some serious baking for my orthodontist's staff when this whole saga is over. They've earned it. I have run into every possible complication with my braces, yet they have maintained an encouraging façade no matter what I've dumped on them. I suspect they draw straws in the back room to see who has to work on my mouth every month. I'm telling you that braces would try the patience of Jesus. No kidding.

If you are thinking about braces yourself, let me reassure you that they are much better these days. They still hurt. Eating is still tricky. They cost the earth, but, other than that, the whole thing is pretty tolerable. By far the worst part is the check-writing. The next-to-worst part is the lisp. The orthodontist's staff claims they can't hear a thing. They're in league to maintain a smiling denial no matter what I complain about. "Yeah, right," I snort. It's 8:30 a.m., and I've already been asked to take a Breathalyzer test. The whole world thinks I have a drinking problem thanks to my new speech impediment.

It better be worth it. That's all I have to say. When the suffering and check-writing are over, I better have a smile that will stop traffic. Otherwise, somebody is going to hear about it.

Hair of the Man

You probably can't tell from the stunningly attractive picture of me on this book cover—we've positioned the lighting just right; the good magicians at John F. Blair, Publisher, work wonders with Photoshop—yet tragically, follicle by follicle, I am losing my hair.

There's a reason I prefer balcony seats.

Now a lot of guys try to be cute about losing their hair. I've seen some T-shirts that read, "It's not a bald spot, it's a solar panel for a super sex machine." Whatever.

Make light if you will. It's traumatic. Ladies: imagine your boobs fell off. This is serious.

Male Pattern Baldness (MPB) is a scientific, hereditary condition, wherein a man's hair falls out, starting in most cases from the crown of said male's head, as a result of having more testosterone than the average guy. And this super-testosterone fellow, if not kept in check by the hair gods who remove a few strands for modesty and character, would probably go on to lead a fast life, running amuck, drinking, flirting, and swearing in the company of his cronies. No, wait a minute. That's what

I do now, so it must be the other way around: men with lots of hair are boring.

What is hair anyway? Archaeologists and anthropologists, aka people who look at rocks all day, believe that the hair on the top of our heads protected us from the crashing blows of enemy clubs back in prehistoric times. Unfortunately, unless you use Kevlar shampoo, I doubt your hair will do much to protect you from modern weaponry. I might be wrong, here. There are a couple of women in Junior League whose hair could stop bullets—if not entire squadrons of Patriot missiles. But I digress.

A bald man can therefore be proud that his ancestors were obviously charming, muscular, powerful, and intelligent enough not to need hair. The hairy, knuckle-dragging, club-toting Cro-Magnons out there knew not to mess with the BALD ONE.

This is not to say that watching your hair wash down the drain does not cause a certain amount of trauma. It is some cruel, cosmic prank that right about the time a guy's skin clears up, his hair begins to fall out. I do remember, however, about six good months in there somewhere.

So it isn't that hard to understand why for centuries, men have rubbed snakeskin, tobacco, coffee grinds, lark's vomit, toothpaste, cooking sherry, formaldehyde, and egg yolks on their heads.

Nor are wigs and funny hats a new thing. Great men in history have lost their hair. For fun, read the following list of names to your friends and ask, "Wig or no wig?" Burt Reynolds, William Shatner, Martin Van Buren, Jefferson, Madison, Michael Jordan, Old Hickory, the Pope (hey—why the big hat?), Genghis Khan, Noah, George Washington, Barbara Bush, Einstein, Marv Albert, Sean Connery, Kojack, Louis XIV, and Yule Brynner.

If you guessed Marv wears a wig, you're wrong. He told Barbara Walters, "It's a weave." Huge difference. Throw some talc on that thing and invite Marie Antoinette over to dinner.

Some friends asked me, "Doesn't it bother you that you're

losing your hair so young?" No, not really. It bothered me at
twenty-one, though.

There I was, combing what used to be a fine head of
thick blonde curls (actually, I wasn't so much combing as I was
merely trying to thwart its advance using a whip and a desk
chair). Then I noticed something. You guessed it; I noticed my
scalp. I'd never seen it before. Yet suddenly there it was, smiling through my haircut.

I called my grandfather.

My grandfather has a cue-ball head. The top is down for a
sunny drive. The eagle has landed on the egg planet. A chrome
dome. Defoliated. *Sans cheveaux*. Folicularly impaired. The
man is bald. And has been bald for over sixty-five years now.

"What kind of hair did you have before it fell out?" I
asked.

"Well, let's see now. Let me think. You know, I believe it
was just like yours," Granddaddy said.

My fate was sealed that afternoon in my college dorm
room. Doom. Calamity. Remorse. I saw the future and it was a
gleaming cupola adorned with nothing. Suddenly, modern fix-
its didn't look so irrational.

"Well, he's not just the president, he's a member," I found
myself saying to my family.

"Minoxidil might work—it was invented in France. How
many bald French guys do you know of other than Voltaire?" I
asked my friends.

"Okay, so let me get this straight. You cut out flaps in
my head and then stretch the hairy part over the top? Is that
legal?"

"If you catch it at the right angle, it's like rows of corn."

"Turkish, wall-to-wall, or Oriental?"

"Do you have that enamel in a lighter shade?"

"Maybe I can grow this one hair long enough to cover all
the space on my head."

I almost succumbed to those traps, but thankfully my
grandfather saved me. Did he need a toupee when blasting the Germans to Kingdom Come in the Big One? Did my

great-grandfather, General John Morgan, need to check his comb-over when he had his horse shot out from under him at Chickamauga? Did my great-great-grandfather, the Right Rev. Morgan, blubber and question the Almighty when he found a hairball in the tub back in 1791?

They did not. And if bald is good enough for them, it's good enough for me.

Chapter 13

Fa So La Ti Da

Tips from a Soprano

For a brief hour or two every Wednesday night during choir practice and a fleeting hour-and-a-half on Sunday mornings, I am more than just a Southern woman. For those hours, I am: a soprano. I love singing in my church choir. It's the only thing I do on a regular basis simply for fun. It's challenging, and I work hard at it, which brings us to my first tip. Singing is rarely a mandatory activity for adults. Remember that. When is the last time you witnessed a full-grown adult being wrestled to the ground and forced to sing something from *The Sound of Music*? I'm a soprano, but I don't think I'm a Julie Andrews soprano.

If you really and truly can't sing, just say no. If you decide to sing in a choir, pay attention to the choir director. If you think your director is trying to tell you something with his or her eyebrows, you're probably right. Choir directors have very expressive faces. Also, if fellow singers play "Rock, Paper, Scissors" to see who has to sing by you, you may want to check your pitch. When someone offers to highlight your part for you, you can safely assume you have stepped on another singer's lines. Worst of all, if you've been out of town for a few weeks, and on your return, the rest of the choir seems a wee bit disappointed to have you back, you might want to take it down a notch. In a choir, blending is good. If you really have no vocal talent, you should bring delicious baked goods to practice. Bribery is an ancient and venerable art. It still works. If your voice is good, but singers on either side of you still lean away from you like overblown tulips, you may need to pop a breath mint. Your biggest problem may not be your high notes. It may be the garlic cheese dip you scarfed down at lunch.

If you really like to sing, even though you can't carry a tune in a bucket and everybody knows it, go ahead and go for it—in an appropriate venue. The shower in your bathroom is the perfect spot. Another good idea is to sing your heart out in the closed confines of your own automobile. If it's dark outside, you can belt out a full-bodied rendition of *Aida*, and no one will see, hear, or suspect a thing. Go ahead and conduct the orchestra with one hand, if you feel the urge, but, in the interest of public safety, I urge you to keep one hand on the wheel. I am quite certain there have been interstate pileups caused by someone getting carried away while singing in the car. Just because nobody wants to admit that to a police officer doesn't mean it hasn't happened, you know.

Another piece of advice is that if you can't sing, but you feel moved to sing anyway in the spirit of public unity, civic-mindedness, or some such patriotic notion, here's a hint: sing *softly*. It's not in your best interest to overpower those around you who really can sing. If you sing softly enough, you'll enjoy it. You'll be one of the gang—like you really belong in the whole singing milieu—with people who can sing the "Hallelujah Chorus" with ease, people who use words like *milieu*. The best part about singing softly is that no one will actually know you can't sing because they won't be able to hear you. Sensitive ears may hear something a little off, but they'll be stumped when they try to identify the off-key chorus member. Sure, they may suspect something. It's hard to hide a tone-deaf voice, even in a crowd. An off-key note rips across a room like bird shot across a cow pasture. If you hear whispers along the lines of, "Did you hear that?" just shrug your shoulders along with everyone else. Nobody can prove a thing.

Another tip is to be a good listener. There is nothing more musically appealing to a talented singer than a good listener. Everybody loves an audience. We can't all be stars. Somebody has to applaud. Be the best clapper out there. Cheer. Let 'er rip with the occasional wolf whistle. Flatter the singers around you. Praise their high notes. Everybody has a part to play. Maybe your role is to be the appreciative audience. Go with your strengths.

One other tip is to accept the gifts you were born with. Your voice is what it is. You are stuck with whatever talent God saw fit to give you. Nothing you can do will really change that. Of course, you can train and stretch that talent. The musical choices you make with regard to repertoire—all of those variables are up to you. Just don't expect to make it to La Scala if you don't have the pipes, no matter how much you practice. That's all I'm saying.

Ironically, some people have beautiful voices, but they are afraid to use them in public because they are unwilling to make mistakes. Great singers go for broke. They take a chance and put themselves out there on the edge. Sometimes, those singers are the toast of the town. On other occasions, they stink it up. You have to be willing to read the reviews. This inability to risk it all is a total waste of talent, in my opinion. The good news is that if you have a so-so voice, you can gin it up a letter grade or two with the correct control, practice, clever music selection, and sheer nerve and force of will.

In the end, however, singing stars are born with a certain *Je ne sais quoi* that puts them in a separate category from the rest of us. Once you hear one of these natural talents sight-read a piece of music perfectly—something you've been struggling with for weeks just to get it to a non-embarrassing level—well, it's enough to send you to the back row of the choir with your sheet music crumbled into a ball and stuffed in the bottom of your church pocketbook.

Learn to live with what you've got. Improve what you can.

Memorize your music like it's Mao's *Little Red Book*, and you are a dedicated communist party member. Cover up what you can't fix, and, finally: don't volunteer for solos. This brings up an important point that you wouldn't think I'd have to mention. This should be a no-brainer. Alas, some people just seem to be thick as a plank. If you can't sing and everybody knows it, for goodness sake: *don't volunteer to sing a solo.* You need a buddy for anything more complicated than a commercial jingle. I know most of you are just baffled that I feel the need to spell this out, but you would be amazed at the things some people volunteer to do in public—regardless of talent or ability. Have you ever watched the tryouts for *American Idol*? I can't bear to watch myself. I am embarrassed FOR some of those people.

A little warning here: beware of people who volunteer to sing solos. This could be an iffy thing. It is a strange fact that some of the best singers in the world have to be coaxed into starring roles, and some of the worst singers in the world have to be beaten back with a broom. I can't explain this phenomenon, but it is nothing new. Ask any choir director. He or she will tell you that I speak the truth. The world is apparently loaded with would-be soloists.

One strategy for those who cannot sing is to pretend. Faking it can be good. I am generally against lying in most situations, except when the truth will hurt someone's feelings unnecessarily, in which case a little white lie won't hurt a thing. This is one such exception. A little pretense here is the polite thing to do. Nice manners require the occasional fib. If you really can't sing, a gracious way to participate in Christmas caroling without actually singing is to move your lips along with the words. You will seem mysterious. No one will know for sure. Keep your game face on. Admit nothing. Smile benignly at the crowd and glide gracefully—do not run—to the closest exit.

As a last-ditch measure, if you can't sing a lick, I recommend that you stand really close to a first-rate singer who is raising the roof. When necks stretch from all directions to try and identify the wonderful voice, nod modestly and accept the smiling accolades as if you have, indeed, been "discovered." Modesty is, occasionally, overrated.

If you are a first-rate soprano, please sit by me. If you are not, well, I'd appreciate it if you'd move on up to the balcony. I have to concentrate on the soprano line, and, quite honestly, I can't handle too many distractions.

Bass Observations

~ **M**usic and singing should fill your life daily. Don't save the gift of song just for holidays, baseball games, and church.

My mother, a Southern lady and operatic soprano with a voice straight from heaven, can play any instrument, made up songs for me when I was a little boy, and sang me to sleep every night when I was growing up. Mama introduced me to melody, harmony, and instruments—notice I said "introduced," not "made me best friends with." I appreciate gorgeous voices like my mother's. It isn't Christmas Eve until Mother sings "O Holy Night." If our family were a musical troupe, Mama would be the star attraction, the main gig, the one people pay the big bucks to hear. Growing up, I took her for granted, mistakenly thinking everyone's mother could do the same thing.

As our family's musical leader, Mama wanted all four of her children to sing and develop an ear for song. Thus, we were all relegated to instruments. In the second grade, I was given the cello to master.

Let me tell you something about the cello: it is a fine instrument, full of grace and beauty, as long as you are playing with other people. The cello is not something you play by yourself. *In situ*, it supports an entire orchestra. Solo, it sounds like a dying cow. Even Yo-Yo Ma has trouble making the cello sound great as a solo instrument. You don't sit down and strum out a little cello ditty. Few enjoy listening to a cello concert. You can't play "Happy Birthday To You!" on the cello or anything else upbeat. Pretty college girls don't wait to be serenaded by a dude with a cello. Friends don't gather 'round the cello for some beer-hall singing. No, the cello best lends itself to funeral dirges and support for more ornamental instruments such as the violin and trumpet.

Worse, my cello teacher frightened me. In retrospect, I'm sure she was a nice woman, but at the time, I thought of her as Old Lady Matheson, leader of the Birmingham Musical Inquisition. She was always asking me tough questions such as, "Did you practice?" (No.) "Did you learn this piece?" (Are you kidding me?) "Do you recognize the fingering here?" (Absolutely not.) "Do you know which end of this instrument is up?" (Not really.)

I'd desperately saw out my assigned pieces and be greeted with, "That was a disgrace to Mr. Bach." (I agree.)

The truth is, I loathed the music. Bach bored a young boy who preferred running around in the woods with a slingshot. Then one day in the third grade, my friend Atkins pounded out "The Pink Panther" on the piano in music class. Now that was *cool*. "Where'd you learn that?" I asked. "From my music teacher!" Atkins replied cheerily. "Man," I thought, "you can learn that from your music teacher?" I thought music teachers only assigned pieces written by the Three Bs: Bach, Beethoven, and Blech.

That Tuesday at my weekly lesson, I asked Old Lady Matheson if I could play "The Pink Panther" on the cello. "That is not music," she replied, and handed me another score by the powdered-wig set. That taught me lesson one: don't be a musical snob.

My tortured relationship with Old Lady Matheson lasted a few more years. She thought I didn't like to practice. I thought she had a music stand up her butt. Mother called an end to my cello career when I was in the fifth grade, disappointed that I had given up on music.

Yet that same year, I appeared onstage with Mama as Buttercup's assistant in the Birmingham Civic Opera's production of *H.M.S. Pinafore* by Gilbert and Sullivan. That minor performance changed my life.

I really enjoyed singing. Gilbert and Sullivan were funny guys. I told my friends back at school about the plot: how the captain was swapped with the lowly deckhand at birth and then married his nanny. Hilarious! The guys in fifth-grade gym class looked at me blankly. A galactic wedgie taught me not to share G&S jokes with the general public.

So I sang in church, with my family, and at the occasional birthday party. I did not sing around friends or in a setting where other people weren't singing. In college, my best friends were in a band that sang folk music. Aside from the fact that there were no preppy Republican protest songs for me to warble, everyone assumed I didn't sing anyway, so I never joined the band. I missed out on a lot of fun there.

When I moved to New York after college, I happened to be at a cocktail party one night with a Southern woman named Angela Cason. Angela asked me what I wanted to do while I was in the city. Flippantly, I replied that, "I've always wanted to sing *H.M.S. Pinafore* in Carnegie Hall."

"I think I can help you with that," Angela replied. You see, Angela belonged to the Blue Hill Troupe, an opera group dedicated to performing Gilbert and Sullivan in New York City for charity. Six months later, I found myself in Carnegie Hall, singing *Pinafore* with Skitch Henderson and the New York Pops. My mother sat in the balcony, crying, probably, at the injustice in the world that her son, a hack, could be on that stage.

While in that performance, I spotted a pretty, brunette soprano in the chorus and heard her gorgeous voice. It took a few months, but once I found the nerve to ask her out, we became an item and eventually, the 127th marriage to come out of singing Gilbert and Sullivan in the Blue Hill Troupe. I'd found Mrs. Murphy through the gift of song.

An accomplished opera singer trained in vocal performance at Juilliard and New England Conservatory, my wife's voice and training puts me to shame. She has sung all over the world. I have sung all over the house. She reads music. I read *The Wall Street Journal.* She speaks five languages so she can sing with the proper emotion in German, Italian, French, Latin, Spanish, and English. I speak English (kinda). Her personal singing mantra involves being an "intelligent singer" with breath support and proper warm-ups before every performance.

My personal singing motto is, "Strong and wrong, loud and proud."

In retrospect, I worried for too many years that I couldn't sing. I worried that my musical taste was geeky or somehow not cool enough for public consumption. I worried that if I tried to sing harmony in church, the choir might boo. I worried that no girl would ever enjoy hearing my voice sing out a song to her. For most of my life, I sang softly. I lip-synched. I avoided calling attention to myself.

Then, thankfully, I grew up and found some courage, found my own voice. I decided I didn't care what others thought about my music choices, that by damned, I hated the thought of wearing flowers in my hair to San Francisco. I auditioned for solo parts with the Blue Hill Troupe and had a blast playing villains and old people. (Basses are always relegated to playing bad guys and the elderly in G&S. Those high-flying tenors get the girl.) I thundered away in church, bellowing our Presbyterian dirges from the balcony, which seem to always be written in the key of gloom. The choir can go stick it, for all I care. God said, "Make a joyful noise," not, "Try to sing round shapes, put your tongue by your teeth, and pull that F-sharp up a half step."

Today, I sing at parties, at weddings, at Japanese karaoke joints, in the car, on the street, digging in the garden—everywhere. I sing to my wife, my mother, my grandmother. I sing all the time because life is worth singing about.

Some say, "Dance like nobody is watching."

I say, "Sing like nobody is listening."

Chapter 14

Gadgets and Gizmos

New and Improved

I love new inventions. I feel an urge to buy every new gizmo that promises to make my life easier, cleaner, more organized, simpler, or more fun. I have to really restrain myself from ordering gadgets advertised on late-night television. My bedside-table drawer has a notepad with scores of 800 numbers—just in case I decide to take advantage of a limited-time, limited-quantity, once-in-a-lifetime offer.

I remember when connecting to the Internet in the privacy of my own home via a wireless laptop seemed about as likely as contacting extraterrestrial life. Now, I'm irritated if my e-mail server goes down for an hour. I no longer find it remarkable that I can shop online in Hong Kong for a new bathrobe that will be tailored to my personal fat rolls and shipped within twenty-four hours to my home address.

In my life here in America, I rarely stop to think about—much less marvel over or rave about—the fact that I can buy and sell stocks in euros or yen from my laptop. Okay, I admit I've never actually done it, but I could, theoretically, which is the point. I could do this while wearing pajamas and surfing satellite television stations to see what's happening in the farthest corners of the globe. I'm interested. I don't, personally, want to eat the still-beating heart of a cobra, but I admit that I paused with the remote for a few revolting, yet strangely riveting moments the other night to watch while someone else did that on television.

Slicing a banana in my kitchen is a technological miracle to me. The banana was grown on another continent thousands of miles away. It's a perishable fruit that was picked green and shipped in giant containers across a vast ocean for me to buy for less than a dollar a pound at my grocery store. Ever thought about that? Go ahead. Take a minute. Bananas and other perishable produce—all timed out to travel from Guatemala to Alabama at just the right time to be consumed with the least spoilage possible. I can't get over it. I can't manage teenagers in my own household without threatening to take away cell phones, but someone, somewhere, can get bananas to the wooden bowl on my kitchen table before they are too bruised or too ripe to eat. That amazes me.

I'm impressed by all kinds of technology. I can repeat, parrot-fashion, how iPods and GPS units work, but I don't really understand it. I have a mystical belief in all things technological. On some level, although I have enough sense not to say this out loud in front of my friends, I believe it's all sorcery. Hocus-pocus. Trickery. It has to be. How can microwaves actually heat up last night's pot roast? I can explain how something works when my children ask (you can look up anything on the computer these days), but I'm really just repeating words I've read.

On a gut level, I believe in everything. Over the years, when my children asked about space aliens, ghosts, the Bermuda triangle, conspiracy theories, reincarnation, God, déjà vu, death, Lady Luck, eternity, voodoo, predestination, miracles, magic, microeconomics, holistic medicine, telepathy, time travel, schizophrenia, the chaos theory, where socks go in the dryer, and how to keep Venice from sinking, I'm a frustrating parent because . . . I believe in everything, at least a little bit. That's not very satisfying if you're a kid. Children are not interested in abstractions. They don't want to participate in big-picture, we're-all-connected, meaning-of-life parables.

Explaining how something works is a technological mine-field for parents. You never know when you're going to be asked something important, something you want to answer carefully and thoughtfully. You can bet the farm that you'll be asked such questions when you're shouting your family's hamburger order into the microphone at a fast-food drive-through, or while you are trying to fill out paperwork for someone in the emergency room, or in between bouts of throwing up when you have food poisoning, and your child has decided to sit outside the bath-room door to ask questions-which-cannot-wait. Children pick those moments on purpose. Nobody can lie under that kind of pressure. You say what you really think, what you know, what you wonder about, what you feel, and what you guess. No par-ent in the history of the world has been asked meaning-of-life questions in prearranged, one-on-one quality time while sit-ting on a beach at sunset. That has never happened. It never will.

Just this week, I stumbled across some technological mag-ic that got me pretty revved up. I drive a ten-year-old Suburban with over 280,000 miles on it. It could go at any minute into the giant headlight in the sky. It is full of baseball dents and door dings, a car regularly stuffed to the brim with children, sports equipment, pets, pool toys, potting soil, and garage-sale merchandise.

It has a few quirks. For example, the automatic locks no longer work. I have to slide my fanny onto the console in the middle of the front bucket seats in order to stretch my right arm as far as possible to unlock the front passenger-side door by hand. Recently, I've experienced nagging neck pain. I've just figured out that it is caused by the gymnastic contortions I have to perform to unlock the doors of the car for my children without getting out of the car in the carpool lane at school. (This is forbidden unless you have a child choking to death in the backseat; if you do, it's okay to get out of the car, as long as you don't block traffic or halt the carpool line while you save your child's life.) My old car is literally a pain in my neck. Feel free to yuk it up.

In addition, the turn-signal sound comes on at odd times, spontaneously, of its own free will. I can't turn it off. I can't tell you how much this gets on my nerves. It isn't a steady, monotonous sound. It varies. Sometimes, it blinks a mile a minute like it is Lassie trying to warn me that the bridge is washed out in the road directly ahead of me. At other times, it is half-hearted, like it can't really be bothered to get into a blinker rhythm. The good news is that the blinker problem is only a sound issue; there is no inappropriate blinking visible to other drivers. Inside the car, it is a different story. Passengers frequently scream at me in the middle of a conversation, "Will you *please* turn off that blinker?" I have to explain. While the noise is climb-up-in-a-tower-and-shoot-people annoying to me, it is not actually dangerous. This is important. To avoid a car payment, I will, apparently, put up with all sorts of irritating noises, but I draw the line at actually endangering the general public.

With the inevitable new car threat on the horizon, I stopped by a car dealership in between errands one day and stumbled upon one of my favorite things: a new invention. It was right there at the car dealership in one of the new cars.

I am not exactly a car salesperson's dream buyer. I always have a budget. I'm not really interested in cars, per se, although I have been known to go ape over a new-and-improved cup-holder accessory and an innovative third-seat-removal option. (It takes two high school males with ten inches of height and fifty pounds of weight on me to remove the third seat in my old Suburban when I have to haul things around like a truck driver, something I am frequently called upon to do. The directions in the glove compartment claim: "Easily removable third seat, just grasp the handle and tug!" What a joke. Downright lie is what it is. I couldn't remove that third seat on my own if my life depended on it.) Also, the only option I'm interested in talking about is the air conditioner, and it better be good enough to cool down the space shuttle on re-entry into the earth's atmosphere because I am not fooling around when it comes to air conditioning. I'm looking for top-of-the-line with the AC. I live in the Deep South. As a hormonal Southern woman, I want the best air conditioner money can buy.

Right after I climbed into the driver's seat to try out the air conditioning, I tuned in just long enough to the salesman's spiel to catch something along the lines of ". . . self-parking."

Hold the horses a minute.

"What did you just say? What do you mean 'self-parking'? There's no such thing! You are making that up!" I challenged the salesman. He was hoping to close the deal with the new parking feature, and I was biting. I couldn't help myself. He knew he had me. I gave up parallel parking a decade ago with the birth of my third child and the advent of the giant boat-car into my life. I never had the nerve to parallel park my Suburban. I can't even see the end of it in my rearview mirror. It goes on forever back there.

"Listen here, young man. Do not toy with me. You do not know who you are dealing with. If you are lying to me, I'll write a chapter about you and humiliate you all across the country. You better be telling me the gospel truth," I warned him.

"Oh, it's true. This baby will do all the work. See this screen? You can watch the whole thing. The computer will determine the distance between the cars and parallel park, all by itself," he bragged.

"Let's see it," I demanded. "Park this sucker in between those two Mercedes over there."

"No problem," he said, eager to demonstrate the pricey parking package by squeezing the demonstration car into a parking space designed to hold a mini-hybrid-city-car with room for one flat-chested, model-thin woman to slide between the cars if she turned sideways and sucked in her tummy.

It worked. It really did. That car parked itself. Who knows what's next? Maybe they'll invent a teenager who cleans up his room or hangs up his wet towels without being threatened with bodily harm.

Inventions I Need ASAP

A window partition (like the ones in limousines and police cars) so that I do not have to listen to bickering children or their blaring videos on long car trips

A fresh manicure that can survive unlocking the car door, inserting the key in the ignition, and fastening the seat belt

Something that makes my teenagers hang up their wet towels, change the toilet-paper roll, or bring back my change from a twenty-dollar bill

A control-top undergarment that does not make me feel as if someone is squeezing my bladder like a juicer intent on getting the last ounce of vitamin C from an orange

Attractive landscaping that does not require human maintenance

Dogs that can scoop their own poop

An umbrella that doesn't dump water in my lap when I close it to climb in the car

Man's Four Phases of Technology

I am the president of a technology company, yet I drive a fifty-one-year-old car. I love my iPhone but cool myself during the summertime with a 1916 Emerson electric fan.

I see nothing at all contradictory about those statements. Allow me to explain: you see, men go through phases of infatuation with technology.

Phase I: During this techno-lust phase, men embrace all new technology as superior to what is currently available. The new (and improved) model must be faster, lighter, stronger, and altogether better. The new stereo, the new computer program, the new appliance—we want them all. The old ones get kicked to the curb or to a little sister. During my own techno-lust phase, I saved my allowance and worked at odd jobs, so that I might purchase the Adam II (a computer you've no doubt never heard of) or a genuine *laser* compact-disk player. These purchases cost hundreds of dollars and are now worth exactly Jack squat.

It is during this phase that we men have one weakness that trumps almost every other. We are particularly vulnerable to succumb to the siren song of technology. Some men get stuck in Phase I. Those men are easy to spot. Their base-ments are crammed full of old graphite golf clubs, broken fishing rods, space-age-fabric jackets, mold-resistant sleeping bags, and mountains of hi-fi equipment. They just keep replac-ing and replacing and replacing. Conversation perpetually re-volves around the latest gizmo and gadget. Business types refer to them as "early adopters" and, not surprisingly, love Phase I men.

Men stuck in Phase I have their advantages—stay around one of them long enough and they'll probably cast off plenty of perfectly fine equipment in your direction. They also pos-sess strong diagnostic skills and the ability to fix any technical problems you may have. Not only do they have the talent to hook up the DVR to the LCD TV, they *enjoy* an afternoon spent in the company of wires, cables, and tuner boxes.

Phase II: At some point, many men abruptly leave the happy and expensive confines of techno lust. This departure is usually prompted by a technical failure of some kind. The new five-thousand-dollar television won't talk to the cable box. The new 3G phone can't import the old cell phone's numbers. The call center in Mumbai cannot rid the man's computer of the blue screen of death. The man, seething, resorts to (almost) reading the instructions but then remembers to call his thir-teen-year-old nephew, who is still in Phase I, thereby avoiding such a calamity.

This techno failure causes a man to think, if only momen-tarily, before purchasing an upgrade, improved version, or new model. His wife's phrase, "Our television is *perfectly fine*," may resonate in his head at this moment. Oh yeah, and he has a wife and/or children. This means that the man does not have the time or money to pour into a new cordless-answering-ma-chine system every three to six months.

Purchases of new technology during Phase II are made when and only if the old technology wears out or becomes in-operable. That, or if his Phase I buddies make fun of him while on a hunting trip.

Phase III: This may be the crankiest phase of men and

their relationship to stuff. Phase III men loathe all new advances in technology and regard any improved product with abject suspicion, derision, and generally as a waste of money. Advanced age is usually the trigger for Phase III, whereupon a man looks back and reflects on how much cash he has squandered keeping up with the Jones's gadgets.

Phase III men may become quite ornery. It is not unusual for them to hang out in hardware stores and heckle other Phase I and II men who come in with broken products. "That's your problem right there, boy, it's made of *plastic!*" Anything made of plastic, rubber, or foam is immediately dismissed as suffering from a quality defect and labeled *junk*. Likewise, anything manufactured in China, which includes pretty much everything made after 1990, is also deemed junk.

My grandfather (who is ninety-four) remembers an elderly man who used to visit my great-grandfather's general store to listen to the radio on Saturday mornings. One day, this old-timer pulled my granddad aside and told him conspiratorially, "This radio stuff is a buncha bull. There's a phonograph in there."

I remind Granddad, when he dismisses the "Interweb" as a plaything, that his radio is really a phonograph. This does not amuse my grandfather, but does sometimes get him to grudgingly listen to the advantages of the new product. He'll listen for a few moments and then ask, with a wry look, "Does it run on leaded or the hi-test ethyl?"

Suffice it to say, men in Phase III are liable to use such words as *newfangled*. They pine for the good old days of asbestos brake pads and lead in the paint. Drive up in a shiny new Prius and they may hand you a piece of Wonder to toast up for them.

Phase IV: These are men who are so innately familiar with old technology that they become sort of tech gurus. You see, at some point, all technology becomes cool to men, not just the new stuff. Men are fascinated and often collect odd assorted bits of technology. You might see a broker with a paper stock ticker in his office. Or maybe your dad dug up an old telephone insulator in the backyard and now uses it as a glass paperweight. Some men love shortwave radio or dogsledding, simply for the love of the technology itself. Because only one-in-a-hundred men share their passion, they have to learn a lot about it themselves—thus becoming experts—and this old-technology know-how impresses their friends. And to keep up with servicing their old technology, they often simultaneously embrace new technology—think of the guy that uses his iPhone to take a picture of his drill-bit collection to send to another Phase IV buddy building a Chippendale highboy.

I myself fall into this category, which is why I don't find it at all unusual to check messages on my iPhone while tooling around in my 1958 Cadillac.

Now, how these phases interact often causes friction among men. Many men in Phase III deliberately refuse to use a product as it was designed. For example, my other grandfather, Ray Murphy, was a lawyer. As such, he dictated everything for years. His first Dictaphone was a small instrument that made wafer-thin records of his voice memos. This was very cool stuff indeed to a little boy (pre-Phase I) and old hat to my dad (Phase I).

When my father, who worked for the phone company, bought his first answering machine in 1978, my grandfather used to call and dictate to it. We'd get messages like this: Beep. "Mike, this is your father. Full stop. New paragraph. Your mother and I would like you to come to the country club with us tonight, period. I hope Susan will join us, period. New paragraph. Let us know if you need a sitter for Morgan, comma, or if you'd like to bring him along, period. Hard-carriage return. Love, comma, your father, Ray W. Murphy, Esquire, etcetera."

Of course, at the end of the day, it worked for Ray. And that's more than I can say for half the stuff I buy. Period.

Chapter 15

Embrace Your Inner Foodie

Chocolate, My One True Love

The American Medical Association defines all of our addictions as illnesses now. We're not just weak-willed people anymore, in case you haven't heard, which is fabulous news. My chocolate obsession is not my fault. It's a genetic predisposition. Who am I to rail against my biological destiny? I love science.

Here's my premise: a perfect bite of chocolate is better than a lover's kiss. I advise you to examine a chocolate bar's label with the same scrutiny you would give to a potential suitor's appearance. Don't be tempted by a pretty package alone. Go for quality ingredients—in chocolate and men. You can buy good chocolate almost anywhere. Sadly, you can't do that with men. For one thing, it's illegal. For another, romantic partners are not as easy to find as fine chocolate. Don't be fooled by mass-produced, brightly packaged chocolate, designed to tempt unsophisticated buyers. Search long and hard for quality with regard to chocolate _and_ men. Be choosy. One bite (of chocolate, of course), and I promise you'll thank me.

Chocolate is consistent. What you see is what you get. Twenty-four hours a day, seven days a week, at a corner news-

stand or in an expensive restaurant, you can always buy chocolate. You can indulge to your heart's—or pocketbook's—con-
tent. If you can somehow manage to combine the two great
loves of your life—your soul mate *and* chocolate—in one evening's entertainment, you've won the lottery. You only get one
or two of those perfect combinations in a lifetime. Indulge
yourself. Commit every second of it to memory so you can enjoy it again later when you recount every detail for me so that
I can enjoy it, too.

For me, chocolate is more than mere dessert. It is much
more than luxurious and flavorful fat grams. Chocolate consumption is bigger than an ordinary, run-of-the-mill, Twinkie
moment of self-indulgent pampering. Chocolate is a point of
view in itself, a *raison d'être*, a philosophical frame of reference
which separates real women who are prepared to wear control-
top undergarments to accommodate their chocolate intake
from young girls who have no idea how many miles they must
walk on a treadmill to burn off the calories from one Snickers
bar.

Chocolate is the primary reason women like me have refrained from committing a whole slew of criminal acts. In my
opinion, chocolate has saved more lives than Sunday school.
Think about it. It's a whole lot better for a woman to bite the
head off a chocolate Easter bunny than, well, any other head
she might be thinking of biting off. A three-layer chocolate
cake for dessert makes all the salads, steamed vegetables,
brown rice, and diet sodas seem worth it. I know this because
I am a chocolate professional.

Trust me when I tell you that milk chocolate is the best.
Dark chocolate is too sophisticated for my palette, too smell-
the-wine-cork showy, and white chocolate isn't chocolate at all.
It's missing the essential ingredient, cocoa, which *makes* the
chocolate *chocolate*. Without cocoa, it's just sugar and milk,
which is a recipe for something else entirely—like vanilla. I
thought everybody knew this, but, apparently, there are still
people out there falling for the white chocolate ruse. Remember: white chocolate *isn't*. White chocolate is false advertising.

It's an old con game. Don't fall for it. Blow right by the dark chocolate and the so-called white chocolate sections, and fill your candy bag up with my personal favorite: milk chocolate.

Remember: true chocolate aficionados are finished with a bag of chocolate—no matter how many ounces of chocolate it contains—when the bag is empty. There is no nightly allotment, no saving some for later. Chocolate is a compulsion that takes a backseat to no addiction—not alcohol, not gambling or drugs—nothing. If there is chocolate in your pantry, you are duty-bound to eat it. If you can't polish it off by yourself, call me. I am always willing to help a friend.

Just in case you have ever wondered about this etiquette question, I want to clear this up right now. If you live in the South like I do, melted chocolate hazards are everywhere. M&Ms DO melt in the hand. I don't know who ever said they don't. I want you to know that a little melted chocolate never hurt anyone. Feel free to lick it right off the wrapper. Just because it is melted doesn't mean it isn't delicious. If there is anything worth sacrificing nice manners for, it's a melted Reese's cup.

For most of my life, I didn't have to worry about dieting. Since I have always had a little chocolate addiction, that was a good thing. Once I turned forty, my unlimited chocolate party ended. I'm not over the disappointment to this day. Limit my chocolate intake? I might as well lie down on a yoga mat and die. "No need to panic," I was reassured by my friends, "all things are possible in moderation."

The first adjustment I had to make to fat-girl world was strictly mental. I was told that I didn't have to totally abstain from chocolate (which is a good thing since there was zero chance of that happening). I would merely have to make chocolate an occasional indulgence. I asked friends for clarification on this point. I sensed some wiggle room in this area, and I was determined to exploit every loophole to its full potential.

When one friend asked me, in an upbeat, encourage-the-mental-patient voice, how many candy bars I would usually eat at one sitting, I was initially confused.

"What do you mean?" I asked.

"If you opened a bag of Snickers bars, for instance, would you eat one or more than one?" she asked, in what I call her reasonable-person voice. I had the feeling that she was about to try and sell me something I didn't want to buy. I felt a tad whiny and fretful just thinking about her question. I smelled a rat.

"One candy bar is a serving, you know, depending on its size. It could even be two servings," she added, trying to cattle-prod me into dialogue I was clearly reluctant to enter.

After looking into the eyes of a woman I've known for nearly twenty years, a woman I consider my friend, I felt sure, suddenly, for the first time, that we could not be part of the same genus species of human being. You know how humans and chimpanzees share something like ninety-six percent of the exact same DNA? You have to admit: that four percent is noticeable. "We must have different DNA," is the thought that kept racing across the news ticker in my mind. This woman and I cannot possibly share the same chromosomal material. I don't just *want* chocolate. I *need* chocolate.

After a few seconds of contemplation, I decided to answer her tricky question this way: "I would probably eat all the candy bars, unless it was something I didn't like," I finally admitted.

I was secretly pleased by my tempered response. My first reaction had been to laugh in her face. Nobody buys that single-serving nonsense—do they? I felt like I'd been put on the spot in front of a classroom of math geniuses and asked to solve a tricky word problem, something like, "Why can't Jane eat all the candy bars? Because John will insist on getting his half. Otherwise, as we all know, Jane would polish off the whole box by herself."

My friend decided to clarify: "Would you usually eat more than one candy bar at a time?" she asked. I think she was trying to shame me into the correct answer. She asked her question in the same voice one would ask, "Well, have you ever thought about having sex with a sheep?"

I'm not totally stupid. I can see a tricky word problem barreling down on me like an eighteen-wheeler as well as anyone else. For her sake, I tried to give her "all things in moderation" philosophy serious consideration. After all, it sounds reasonable. I can see the logic of it with regard to everything in life *except* chocolate.

I took a deep breath before expanding on my previous response: "If it was one of those bags of fun-size bars, I'd eat however many candy bars were in the bag. I think that makes me pretty normal. Don't you?" (I hesitated because I feared entrapment.) " . . . if they were regular, full-size Hershey bars, the package contains six, so I'd eat six. If they were jumbo, movie-size bars, I could only eat two. They're extremely filling. If it was a box of assorted chocolates, with or without nuts, I find that a layer will usually hold me, unless it's a cheap box of chocolates that only has one layer, which makes it, de facto, a single serving. Any more than one layer at a sitting seems gluttonous to me, unless it's a chocolate emergency." (You find out your husband has been cheating on you, or you've unexpectedly and inexplicably grown a new chin, or you've spilled red wine on your recently recovered sofa, for example.)

"Are we on the same page on this, or what?" I asked my friend. I was fed up and ready for some straight talking.

I needed to know the cultural norms, the social parameters regarding chocolate. I was beginning to fear that my interpretation of *single serving* might require some adjustment. I was starting to feel pressure to conform to other people's serving portions, food pyramids, cholesterol levels, calorie assignments, food exchanges, and other unpleasant graphs and numbers. I never have liked numbers. I can tell all by myself when I've had enough chocolate. I don't need to read it on the side of the package.

My friend's face had a pained expression like the time when I showed her my tummy rolls in the women's dressing room to explain why I would not buy the two-piece swimsuit she favored. That was two years ago, and she swears she's not over that vision yet. She should have just taken my word for it that I look better in a one-piece swimsuit with a skirt that looks like something an ice skater would wear in the 1950s. I know what looks best on my body. We've been together in the big dressing room of life for a long time now. My days of tucking in my shirt and wearing a belt are over. Big deal.

"We need to talk about this further," my friend said, in a weary voice like you use when you are about to tell someone that you really think he or she needs to up the dosage on the Prozac.

In my view, chocolate is just God's way of keeping women sweet. I admit I get mean when I've been chocolate-deprived, and you don't want to get between me and the last chocolate heart after Valentine's Day. I'm not proud of this. It's just the way things are.

How To Use Chocolate for Good

You can combine chocolate consumption with other pleasures. For example, you can eat chocolate while shopping for shoes. In my opinion, life does not get any better than that.

I have heard that you can combine chocolate consumption with another of life's great pleasures, but I have never tried it myself. I do way too much laundry for that.

You can eat chocolate while you are waiting for a handsome man to send you a text message, an e-mail, a voice mail, or shares in his stock portfolio—whatever.

You can eat chocolate while you read your divorce papers. It won't change anything, of course, but it can't hurt anything either.

You can eat chocolate while you wait for the timer to go off when you are coloring your hair. Usually, those minutes are just wasted.

You can help your child get over a scraped knee or hurt feelings by giving him or her chocolate. It works much faster than ice, Tylenol, or talking things over.

You can reward yourself with chocolate for exercising when you felt like doing something (anything) else instead.

You can eat chocolate as a substitute for dinner. It's a proven fact that chocolate will make you happier than lima beans.

continued

You can use chocolate to bribe children to practice their multiplication facts, write their thank-you notes, finish their music theory, or to perform other odious tasks.

You can use chocolate to reward toddlers who demonstrate a mastery of the big boy/girl potty. A big jar of M&Ms is perfect for this.

You can eat chocolate as a form of social protest against the media's love affair with anorexic-looking models.

You can purchase gourmet chocolate as a luxury item to help stimulate the economy. It's patriotic.

You can use chocolate as a form of antidepressant to sooth the savage beast within you and prevent you from causing bodily harm to the humans you gave birth to.

Eat, Drink, and Be Manly

Morgan Murphy

While I served as *Southern Living*'s food critic, I visited at least twenty restaurants per month, or 240 restaurants per year. At each, I generally sampled three appetizers, three entrées, and three desserts. Amazingly, I lived.

When people discover I worked as a food critic, they often ask three questions: (1) What is your favorite meal? (2) How do you stay thin? and (3) How do I get that job?

I'll work backwards. I got the job after a few foodies at the magazine tried writing the column. These were serious chefs and graduates of places such as CIA (Culinary Institute of America) and Cordon Bleu. These were people who could braise, flambé, and poach in their sleep, with one spatula tied behind their back. Problem was, a successful restaurant goes well beyond the dishes served. The foodies just tasted the grub. Excellent food is not enough. A great restaurant stands on three legs: food, ambiance, and service. Any one of the legs can be broken, and you'll still go back for more. For example, most fabulous BBQ stands have awful ambiance (think leaning shack from a Tennessee Williams play), yet the very same spots serve excellent food with strong service. Some four-star restaurants have gorgeous atmosphere, inventive dishes, and snobby service. You take the snobby service because the food and surroundings are so pleasant. If, however, two of the legs are broken—if the shack has awful service or the snobby waiter brings you a lousy meal—that restaurant won't be in business long.

So though I possess no formal culinary training, unless you count the time I watched my grandmother make biscuits, I am a pro at reviewing restaurants. How? Eat at 240 restaurants a year, and you'll become a pro, too. In fact, here's a tip: if you want great service at a restaurant, go by yourself, order a lot of items, write things down in a small notebook, and steal the menu. You'll be treated like a prince, I promise.

Some critics have different philosophies about recognition. They want to be fawned over and adored at a restaurant. To me, that taints the results and is fundamentally unfair to the reader. Some critics will write bad reviews. I suppose that's fine if you review every restaurant in town regularly, but few people have ever asked me, "Where's the worst place to eat in Charlotte?" or, "What's the most dismal dish you've been served in New Orleans?" People may be entertained by a negative review, but when they actually use a review to pick a restaurant, they want to know about the best. The food business is hard enough without critics spoiling the broth with needless bitter ink.

To keep thin and maintain my "cover," I often took friends on my trips. I called this group of people the Traveling Stomachs. The Stomachs had three jobs. Job one was to order what I told them to order, which wasn't necessarily what they (or I) wanted to eat. Job two was to eat some of the meal. Job three was to never order the soup (you can't push around soup to make it look as if you've eaten it).

Some Stomachs followed instructions well. Others did not. My friend Jeffrey went with me to Jackson, Mississippi, on one trip and devoured everything at the first restaurant. "Pace yourself, buddy," I said. "Nah," he said between bites, "this is delicious!" An hour later at the second restaurant he ate almost everything on the table, but avoided the salad. At the third restaurant he just ate what he ordered. At the fourth restaurant he pushed food around the plate and told the waiter to bring him a seltzer. On the way to the fifth restaurant for the evening, he cracked and called my wife, "Tell Morgan to stop feeding me!" Jeffrey walked in the front door, sat down, looked at the menu and declared, "This restaurant is craptacular. Nothing here worth ordering."

That is how you become a restaurant critic. (And as an aside, I always knew that if I ate the entirety of any dish at the fifth restaurant of the evening, it must be a winner.)

The Stomachs were useful in helping me stay thin, but so was the following lesson: I discovered that it wasn't three days of binge eating that made me fat; it was the days *after* the trip. My stomach would be stretched to huge proportions, so I'd come home and devour everything. Remember this tip after Thanksgiving and Christmas: it's not what you eat over the holidays—it's what you eat after the holidays.

And I will eat just about anything. Except Jell-O. I can't stand it.

It's hard to believe, but one of America's silliest foods is a billion-dollar industry. It's even harder to believe the various food items that are routinely mixed with Jell-O. Many Jell-O recipes sound like what's leftover after you defrost the refrigerator and find food you haven't touched since Hitler was a private.

Old ladies in the South are particularly fond of making things out of pulverized cow bones. (Well, what do you think makes gelatin firm?) Tomato aspics jiggle beside congealed vegetable salads and fried chicken at nearly every family reunion. I can't explain it. A congealed salad—a waste of food in nearly every language—has only one use, and that is to throw at one's little sister.

A friend's mother was recently seized by *gelatinitis-disgustinus*, which is a cruel and untreatable disease that apparently addled her brain into thinking that a Jell-O salad was an appropriate dish to bring to a potluck dinner. I have also noted that this woman wears white shoes after Labor Day, so her character is already suspect. Nonetheless, her trailer-park creation sounded like something prison chefs might create: pistachio Jell-O, Cool Whip, cottage cheese, pineapple chunks, maraschino cherries, baby marshmallows, and shredded coconut. Pecans are optional. I am appalled to relate that by the end of the potluck, there wasn't a single miniature marshmallow left in the tin casserole dish.

I'll admit that as a child I actually liked Jell-O. In college, my roommate Bing enjoyed swapping the regular Jell-O cubes in the cafeteria with ones he'd made from vodka. Bing really knew how to waste good liquor on the librarians and trigonometry professors. But it was my grandmother that pulled the whopper of all Jell-O recipes.

The setting: I was ten. It was Thanksgiving. I asked for extra "lime" Jell-O congealed salad. Unbeknownst to me, my grandmother must have accidentally snorted gelatin dust because she actually made the following recipe and thought I would like it: Jell-O, chopped onions, daub of horseradish, yellow peppers, white pepper, splash of hot sauce, sour cream, salt, and garlic. Thinking this was my favorite lime dessert, I stuck a big glob of it in my mouth. "How do you like my horseradish congealed salad, Morgan?" my grandmother blurted.

"Ish is very gooth," I replied, as the stuff dissolved my kidneys. When grandmother wasn't looking, I slipped my congealed salad into a houseplant. While I wasn't looking, my mother put her portion on my plate—my own mother! That's when you know it's really bad.

My favorite dish? That's like asking my favorite color. It depends. My favorite color for eyes is blue. My favorite color for teeth is white. I prefer green grass.

It's the same with food. Yet if I had to pick one favorite, it would have to be banana pudding. You see, some people are cake, cookie, and pastry people. They like flake and crunch and powder. I am a pudding, pie, and ice-cream person. I'm in it for the goo.

This has gotten me in trouble from time to time.

For instance, when I got married. My wife's family is from New York. When my mother-in-law was planning our wedding, I informed her that I'd prefer not to have a groom's cake, for the aforementioned reasons. I asked instead for a groom's pudding. Specifically, the banana pudding from a restaurant in Birmingham called Niki's West (not to be confused with Niki's original downtown location, which is not as good).

Niki's West is a dive, no doubt about it. Visitors are greeted with the sign, "To be served: no tank tops, no bare feet, no rollers on head."

Evidently, Niki's had a rash of roller-headed diners at some point in the past.

The restaurant sits across the street from a semi-truck junkyard in an industrial part of town. The parking lot security guard packs heat. The line attendants, all wielding huge slotted spoons, yell, "Serve YOU!" at guests. This can be intimidating, particularly when trying to decide among which four of the seventy-five vegetables and meats you want on your plate (everything that can walk, swim, jump, or fly spread out dead on the steam line). If you hesitate more than a few seconds, they yell, "Serve YOU, ma'am!" I've only seen it once, but one idiotic person continued to waffle between the catfish and the chicken livers to the point that the Niki's West server just bellowed, "MA'AM!" That was DEFCON 6 of the Niki's world. Very embarrassing.

Yet despite its quirks, Niki's makes the world's best banana pudding. It's served warm, sweet, and delicious. And it has just the right amount of goo to banana. This is the pudding I asked for at my wedding.

My mother-in-law, God love her, faithfully found the recipe and reproduced the pudding. She did this despite the fact that (a) she'd never heard of a groom's cake because they don't have that tradition in Yankee Land, (b) she doesn't like bananas, and (c) banana pudding is an ugly blob no matter how you serve it.

Is that love or what?

When they cracked that pudding open at our wedding,

you should have seen the stampede of Manolo Blahniks and Jimmy Choos to the cauldron of pudding. Elegantly attired women were falling all over each other to get a champagne glass full of banana heaven. Men wiped banana pudding off their ties. Children devoured whole vats of the stuff. The wedding cake, which looked beautiful but tasted dustier than Mrs. Haversham's, sat basically untouched the entire evening.

All of this goes to prove that the culinary arts should focus on delighting people, not about employing complicated recipes, bizarre ingredients, or expensive tools.

Put that one in your mold and jiggle it.

Rules for Eating Out

Don't eat seafood in a land-locked state.

Never order beef "well done." You'll receive the worst cut in the kitchen.

Always leave nothing less than a two-dollar tip, even if the meal was just two dollars.

Regard with suspicion the waiter who answers "Everything!" to "What's good on the menu?"

Beware the waiter who asks, "Do you want more water?" Water is free.

Dare to explore the new and unpredictable. The food might be awful, but you'll have a great story to tell.

Chapter 16

The Buck Stops Here

Money Matters

I'm not very good with money. Money requires math. I hate math. Math makes me feel anxious and headachy like I need a prescription for Xanax or a big vodka tonic. Even my decidedly humble checking account seems overly complicated to me. I worry about bouncing a check even when I know there is no chance of that happening. I'm afraid I may bounce a check *accidentally*. Did you know that bouncing a check is a criminal offense? I would be embarrassed to death if I lost my right to vote because I bounced a check to the bug man. Could that happen? I do not know the ins and outs of felony convictions. I don't think anyone could prove malice aforethought on my part. Still, ignorance of the law is no excuse and all that. Who knows? It's worrisome. No matter how hard I try, I cannot picture myself bunking down in the Big House.

I knew early on that I was no math prodigy. In my graduate school interview, I felt the need to explain my poor math scores. "My English scores are good, but my math scores are sub-species," I confessed. The head of the graduate program in English didn't even blink. "Mine, too," he said. "Who cares?" I knew right then that I was on the right career path.

I've never needed anything more than third-grade subtraction skills to balance my checking account. Even so, I gave up trying to reconcile it to the penny years ago. It's not worth spending three days of my life trying to figure out how I could be $12.57 off somewhere. Life is full of little mysteries. I just take the bank's word for it now. That's what banks do best—subtraction. I'm sure someone out there uses deposit slips for something other than jotting down e-mail addresses, telephone numbers, or notes to leave on friends' windshields, but I don't. I know better than to add up the bill or figure out the tip on my own in a restaurant. I make my kids do it. It's like flash cards. I tell them to add up Mama's vodka tonics and throw in a twenty percent tip. In my opinion, this is good parenting. I feel virtuous about it.

It's not as if I can afford to be contemptuous about money. I'm not rich. I have never *been* rich. I'm in no danger of ever *becoming* rich. As we say in the South, I'm not even "well heeled" (translation: can shop wherever, whenever, for whatever), "comfortably off" (translation: can write a check for a new furnace when the old one breaks, on the spot, without crying), or "not hurting for anything" (translation: has a beach house that sleeps twelve comfortably). My favorite description of a super-rich Southern woman goes like this: "Don't worry about Lillian. Her fiancé may have left her at the altar, but she has more money than God, and that's just on her mama's side. She'll be fine."

I'm not going to inherit money, which brings up an important question. Why do rich people always marry other rich people? Isn't that the biggest waste you ever saw? Why don't rich people occasionally marry poor people? That would be a big help.

You guessed it. I didn't marry money either. This is a real tragedy now that I look back on it. Why I did not pay more attention to money when I was dating, I do not know. All that "in love" business—what was I thinking? Pension plans. Health insurance. Trust funds. Life insurance. Would it be so hard to fall in love with someone who has those assets in spades? Back when we were in college, we should have made note cards on those boys just like we did for girls going through rush in our sorority houses. We could have carried them in our evening bags and warned each other off. "Don't fall for that one! I know he's a great dancer and has cute hair, but his mama is a harpy, his daddy is an alcoholic, and he makes Cs in English! That boy is going nowhere!"

What difference does it make now whether or not the cute boy had dimples and kissed like nobody's business? Odds are that boy grew up to add a second chin and love handles to go with his dimples, and he probably never asked his wife to dance again one time after his wedding reception. It is true that good kissers usually remain good kissers for life, and that right there is powerful mojo. However, just because some boy is a good kisser is no reason to go and marry him. The problem with good kissers later in life is that sometimes they pucker up for someone else. That's how good kissers end up. D-I-V-O-R-C-E-D.

None of my children seems to be headed to the NFL, the NBA, or the MLB. Sadly, I haven't invented a cure for baldness or obesity. If I could do that, I'd be sitting pretty for the rest of my life. I've worked as a teacher, a writer, and a mom. None of those jobs pays squat. All my savings for retirement and my kids' educations seem to be in the tank. Thank goodness, I'm a good bargain hunter, and I'm not above a little dumpster diving or side-of-the-road shopping either. I was amused once when a senior citizen backed his car into mine and said he could not pay for the repairs because he is on a fixed income. "Who isn't?" I asked him.

In order to be truly self-righteous about the evils of money, and, Lord knows, I'd certainly prefer to observe the traditional, tasteful, Southern approach to money—to never mention money at all—I'd have to be above such petty discussions because of a private stash in Switzerland or my underwear drawer. I've said it before, and I'll say it again: in order to ignore money as good manners require us to do down here, you have to have much more of it than I have.

Money for its own sake doesn't tempt me. It's just paper. It isn't intrinsically worth anything. It's an idea. We've all agreed that it's worth something, so it is. The more I think about it, the shakier the whole system seems. It's an arrogant premise. Our financial system was designed, primarily, by men. To me, this explains a lot. Women would have set things up differently. My instincts tell me to hide the cash in a mayonnaise jar under the Confederate jasmine bush in my backyard, to slap a swing next to that bush for a little decorative camouflage, and to park my fanny in that swing every night for cocktails and guard duty. While it is true that I wouldn't make any interest on my buried booty, I wouldn't lose any of it either, which is more than I can say about my other investments. Just talking about money these days makes me feel angry enough to sharpen my knitting needles and head up to Washington, D.C. to find someone to poke in the eye.

Women think differently about money than men. For example, what we save by buying a sofa on sale becomes leftover money to buy matching pillows. As a rule, women put a premium on things like life insurance. If the breadwinners in our homes (male or female) swallow a bad oyster and head to the giant sandbar in the sky, we need to know that our kids can still go to college. We demand that our financial institutions live up to their by-God advertising. That's why those of us eking out the grocery budget with black-eyed peas and rice the last week of the month make such sacrifices. We want our pension plans to be there when we need them so that all the months when we said no to vacations, eating out, and movie night to make those payments over the years were worth it in the end. Women like me would be happy if we never had to think about money again. That would be true financial independence.

Fat chance. Until then, I guess we'll keep pocketing the change that falls out when we switch the laundry from the washer to the dryer and shaking those sofa cushions every time we go to the movies. If you have a better plan, I'd like to hear it. I am wide open to suggestions.

It's Not Easy Being Green

Years ago, polite and refined persons refrained from discussing religion, sex, and politics in public conversation. Those who show such restraint in today's world are either mute or don't speak English. Today, everything is on the table. From the president's libido to the political correctness of prayers, once-taboo subjects are considered engaging topics of discourse.

I'm taking my dog, Gilbert, to training class. He and four other pooches are practicing the fine art of obedience. In such a venue, one might expect the dialogue to range from "sit" to "good boy." I anticipated conversational icebreakers at dog-training class to be, "That's a fine dog you have. What's his name?" or, "I'm sorry he piddled on your shoe." I was not expecting one of my classmates to announce that she'd had a hysterectomy, adding, "I'd recommend it." Other classmates soon piped up with their various operations, and I felt some peer pressure to relay a malady or two of my own. Hmm. I began to contemplate: open with the prostate joke or the recent case of athlete's foot? Thankfully, I came to my senses in time and remarked that Gilbert didn't like the thunderstorms that had moved in the night before. Everyone immediately chimed

209

in that their dogs hated thunder, too, and I avoided breaking any HIPAA laws.

Though most have succumbed to discussing religion, sex, and politics everywhere, all the time, there's still one sacred subject left in the South. One subject that causes little old ladies to titter and twitter and tsk, tsk, tsk. That subject is money.

Mum on money: it's one of the longest unbroken rules of Southern society. "Never let them know how much money you have," was one of my grandmother's primal lessons. Most of my life I've taken that to mean I should be the best-dressed gentleman in debtor's prison. Still, I don't think that's what she meant. It was her habit to only buy a new car once every three presidential administrations. Carpets in her house were threadbare. Old dresses and handbags were "perfectly fine." A five-dollar birthday gift was considered extravagant. As a child, I thought seeing the road pass beneath my feet as I looked through my grandmother's car's floorboards was an optional accessory from Chevrolet. I remember she traded that car when the back door came off in my grandfather's hand. "Use it up, wear it out, make it do, or do without," was a moral imperative, not a result of our economic circumstance.

I think Grandmama's aversion to flashing cash dated to the "Late Unpleasantness" (as she referred to the War Between the States). After the war, the only people with any money in the South were carpetbaggers or scalawags—i.e., strangers to the South or those who had sold out the Cause. That turned Southern society upside down. Fine old families with long Southern lineages were broke. Upstarts were loaded. So if and when a formerly well-to-do family did manage to scrape together a few nickels or dig up the family silver, they didn't talk about it for fear of being labeled as a traitor.

That tradition lingered in my hometown, Birmingham, Alabama. Birmingham is a "Buick town." For years, no matter how successful you became, how much you earned, or where your social status registered, it was considered well and proper to drive a Buick. The mayor drove a Buick. Head ministers drove Buicks. The CEOs of the biggest banks and businesses all piloted Buicks. Granted, these were top-of-the-line Buicks: Park Avenues and Electras. Underlings drove LeSabres or Centuries. Moms drove Estate Wagons. But they were still Buicks. One or two flashy doctors drove foreign cars. Retired persons might have Cadillacs. I loved those snazzy automobiles, but my fellow townspeople mostly talked ugly about their drivers as, "having something to prove," or people who "probably bought those cars on time." The worst insult was, "That family has more money than sense."

I thought having more money than sense sounded like a fantastic affliction. Rich and dim seemed, to my reasoning, like a happier existence than brilliant and broke. We never said the word *rich*, however. The substitute word for *wealthy* in Birmingham is *nice*. So when someone in the 'ham is said to come from a *"nice* family," that means they make a lot of money. If someone refers to your family as "fine," it's generally accepted that you live off your investments. "New money" spent cash lavishly where people could see it: cars, art, and gadgets from Sharper Image.

So, having grown up in this coded atmosphere of measured restraint, imagine my first day working as a reporter for *Forbes* magazine. I was hired by Jim Michaels, the diminutive but wildly frightening editor-in-chief who had broken the news of Mahatma Ghandi's assassination and ruled *Forbes* with a mighty pen. Michaels could edit the Lord's Prayer down to six words and you wouldn't miss anything. The day I started, most of the reporters were assigned to fact-checking the magazine's annual "Rich List." Michaels told me to call Donald Trump and confirm how much money he raked in the year before.

"I can't do that," I responded.

"Why not?" Michaels barked.

"Because I'm from the South and we don't ask people questions about money," I replied.

"Then you're fired," my boss glowered.

"Let me get Trump on the line," I said.

To my great surprise, Trump was the first of a long line of business people, celebrities, and politicians who willingly shared their incomes and net worth. Some would even fax in their tax returns to the office. I could not believe their candor. After years of being mum on money, I felt like an Amish kid in a Radio Shack.

Plus, it was fun. "Nice" people in my hometown bought Buicks and ate at cafeterias. That's how they stayed rich. Rich folk in New York drove Ferraris and ate in restaurants that sounded like Middle Eastern potentates and terminal illnesses: Balthazar, Chez Panise, and La Goulue to name a few.

They bought stuff, too. The Forbes family had yachts; a helicopter; a DC 9; a townhouse crammed with Cezannes, Monets, and Renoirs; cars; motorcycles; a French château; and a bottle of wine that belonged to Thomas Jefferson. Malcolm Forbes collected tin soldiers. The man had a whole army, navy, and air force of tin men, which is incidentally a line he used when he lured former secretary of defense Casper Wineberger to join the magazine, "Cap, you can have your own army and never have to go to congress for appropriations."

I imagined the wildly rich to be bonkers. That was another legacy of my Southern upbringing. If you're *crazy* in the South, that means you're broke. *Eccentric* is a word only applied south of the Mason-Dixon line to monied people, such as the ninety-four-year-old spinster in my hometown who redecorates the country club hot pink every year on her birthday.

Yet to my surprise, I found most of the rich people I talked with at *Forbes* to be completely normal. They were polite, caring, and interesting. Many gave millions away to charity. Over eighty percent of them were self-made. Most of them still worked— not for the money, but because they loved to, well, work. One retired executive said to me, "When I was poor, I couldn't even help myself. Now I can help thousands of people."

The episode caused me to go back and read Timothy 6:10, which I'd remembered as, "Money is the root of all evil." (Hey, I'm Southern. Bible verses get thrown around a lot down here.) That's only half of the verse, however. The other bit, which is often conveniently left off, is "For the *love of* money is the root of all evil: which while some coveted after, they have erred from the faith, and pierced themselves through with many sorrows" (italics mine, not God's). The root of all evil was the love of money. Not the love of work. Not the love of success. Not the love of earning money. But simply coveting other people's wealth.

It was a pretty tall order not to covet those who made $12,000 an hour when I made a mere $12,000 a year. Yet the more rich people I met, the more their reality contrasted with the media's view of wealthy people: money grubbing, evil, Scrooge-like fat cats who were somehow crooked.

Popular culture today continues to pillory rich people—they're an easy target and a small minority. *Social justice* is a term used by a lot of well-intentioned folks, but to me the phrase threads a dangerous needle with a mixture of envy and righteous populism, and I remember to try not to become fixated on what others have that I don't.

There was a preacher in Boston, Reverend Ike, who sent a monthly magazine to me called "Right Now!" I was a subscriber for years. Rev. Ike mostly preached about money, wealth, and how to get rich—the main secret of which seemed to be sending money to Rev. Ike. I liked Ike for his gift of headlines such as, "Rev. Ike Prophesied and Even Her DOG Became a Millionaire!" Sometimes the magazine came with free "prayer oil" or "money hands," which have not helped my bank account as of yet, but I'm still hopeful. Ike wrote, "The BIBLE said that it's easier for a camel to get through the eye of a needle than a rich man to get into heaven. So think how hard it must be for a poor man to get in!"

I'm no Biblical scholar, but at face value, that strikes me as a sketchy interpretation. Still, it may have some merit: rich is a state of mind. I've met people in the halls of power who commanded huge bank accounts but were utterly broke, busted, and bankrupt. Similarly, I've stumbled across destitute beggars who are rich beyond measure.

Money? Maybe we should talk about it.

Chapter 17

The Not-So-Great Outdoors

Yard Work is for Men

I thought I made my views perfectly clear on this subject to everyone—family members, friends, neighbors, and perfect strangers walking past my house who have the temerity to ask me to my face about the sad state of my ancient flower beds. The truth is that I do not do yard work. Period. End of discussion. Yard work makes me feel "hard done by." This expression is something we say in the South that means "put upon" or "taken advantage of." Feel free to use it yourself, no matter where you live. It is most effective if followed by a deep sigh that further emphasizes one's long-suffering state.

Whenever I am forced to wade through piles of moldy leaves in expensive suede shoes to get to my car, or when I am tempted to hack a path through the monkey grass in my backyard with a machete to take out the garbage, I feel cranky and fretful, like a toddler who has just spiked a fever, because I fear I may be conscripted into seasonal yard work like a member of a jailhouse chain gang.

I tried it. I hated it. The Lord knows that I tried hard. (This may, in fact, sum up my life. I fear that my epitaph may read: "Here lies Mel. She tried hard.") I'm not good at yard work. I'm not educated for it. I don't enjoy it. There are a million things I'd rather do than yard work. I'd rather get my teeth cleaned. I'd rather scrape cat throw-up off the carpet. I'd rather defrost the freezer and throw away unidentifiable leftovers. I'd rather unclog a toilet stopped up with Barbie heads. (It's a long, strange story. It happened years ago. We do not have time for it here.)

I have always been under the impression that one of the many benefits of marriage is that I get a free yardman thrown in with the ring. Was I wrong in this assumption? I thought it was one of the marital trade-offs. I do all the gift-wrapping in exchange for yard work. I don't know about your relationship, but my marriage contains a number of intricately balanced bargains like this one, a practice I highly recommend to any of you just-married folks. For example, my husband is responsible for killing any bugs which happen to wander into our hacienda. He agreed to this deal speedily when I offered, in exchange, to launder all the linens when one of our children vomits in bed. This arrangement is tailored to meet our personal needs. Feel free to work out your own bargains. Successful marriages are full of compromises. Remember: you heard it here first.

What I despise most about yard work is that it is never-ending. As soon as you rake up and bag the leaves, more fall from the tree, often while you are still raking. Just a week or so after you mow the lawn, it needs to be cut again. I already wash four loads of laundry a day. I don't need any more jobs.

Also, yard work defies Mother Nature, which seems wrong to me on a fundamental level. Picking up sticks out of the yard strikes me as unnatural. The yard is where sticks are supposed to be, is it not? Tell the truth: if you find a stick inside your house, what are you going to do with it? You're going to chunk it out the front door into the yard, right? The whole manicured-yard obsession is beyond my understanding.

I respect Mother Nature. I don't make a mortal woman mad if I can help it. Tweaking Mother Nature's handiwork is not on my to-do list. I don't want to get her stirred up. It seems wrong to me to try and make living things conform to my landscaping whims. I'm having enough trouble rearing the children I gave birth to. Children aren't born with nice manners, you know. It takes years of cultivation. You have to weather some serious storms. There are numerous disappointments along the way. Sometimes, you have to prune children's branches. We all know you are legally required to feed and water children, but they also crave your undivided attention, all your free time, every dime you can scrounge up, and the patience of a saint to come into fruition. Children are more trouble than orchids and roses, and that is saying something. Parenting, like plant cultivation, is a long-term venture. I just hate that. Don't you? I wish parenting involved more instant gratification. Then I wouldn't have to say to my children, "I don't care what you think about my parenting right now. Come back when you're forty, and I'll listen to anything you have to say."

I've spent years fighting the ivy on the outside of my house. It wants to eat my brick. It's very strong-willed. It sneaks its tentacles underneath the windows in my dining room (which are painted shut, so I don't see how this is possible) to stretch longingly toward my grandmother's china cabinet. I have actually pruned the ivy IN my dining room in addition to the ivy growing outside the windows. That ivy may be the only thing holding my old house together. The mortar looks mighty thin.

I don't have an instinct for plants like I do for cooking or parenting or writing. The things I don't want to thrive—like weeds, kudzu, poison ivy, and acorn sprouts—grow like they're on steroids, no matter how much I weed them out, spray them with environmentally unfriendly pesticides, or curse them into oblivion. The plants I fret over prayerfully with vitamin-laced rainwater, fertilizer, special stakes, warm blankets, and lulla-bies—*those* plants fall over and die at the drop of a hat. I think it is pure spite.

Every season, I fall in love with one potentially fabulous plant—a perfect hydrangea, a full-color illustration of paper-white bulbs, a field of imaginary lilies, or a basketful of hypo-thetical zinnias. Every single year, my hopes are dashed. It's always something. One time, I planted the bulbs too deeply.

Another time, I planted the bulbs upside down. Picky, picky. If a breech baby can make it into the world, surely a paperwhite can work its way up to the sun. Another excuse: too much rain. Then, there was a drought. A hard freeze got the buds one year. Grubs. Bugs. Mites. Mold. Basketballs. Yes, basketballs. The basketball goal in our backyard is bordered by flower beds. A lack of rebounding on the part of teenagers has beheaded more flowers than a French guillotine. Apparently, it would be easier for me to get into the Kingdom of God through the eye of a needle than it is for me to grow a bouquet of flowers big enough for my dining table right here in Alabama. I am fed up with the whole thing.

The only part of yard work that I'm really interested in is the potential yield: flowers. To capture my interest, a plant must bloom. Sure, I also require the occasional bit of greenery for flower arranging, plants like eucalyptus and acuba, but you can throw all the boxwoods into the Grand Canyon for all I care. There is nothing more boring, in my opinion, than anything that qualifies as a hedge.

I've loomed over many a planter deliberating its occupant's fate.

"Should I pull you up?" I think to myself, "You should have bloomed by now if you were going to do anything. You had two whole years, and I haven't seen one thing from you."

I imagine my flowers responding, "No need to be hasty! I was just about to show you something special. Give me two more sunny mornings and a light rain. I'm planning a little something on my left side that is going to knock your socks off."

Sometimes, I reach down, yank that plant out by the roots, and replace it with something else on the spot. Other times, I grant it a temporary stay of execution, take my clippers, and move on. It's good to let plants know you have your eye on them. It motivates them to quit fooling around and bloom. Use it or lose it is what I say about the limited space in my flower beds.

The only other thing about yard work that interests me is

the accessories. My particular weakness is large-brimmed gardening hats. I never saw one, old or new, that I didn't want to try on to see how captivating it might make me look. I love how gardening hats provide shade for my complexion. I am over my sun-worshiping days. I have no desire to court skin cancer or wrinkles. I also like to have an assortment of gardening gloves. I like old toile patterns best. I've never met a toile fabric I didn't love. My friend has promised to bury me in the toile drapery fabric in her bedroom, which is really sweet of her, considering how much that fabric costs per yard.

Best of all, I love my genuine, sweetgrass flower-gathering basket from South Carolina. I watched a woman in a Charleston market finish weaving this basket herself. Sadly, basket weaving is a dying art. In my mind, I bought a piece of history when I wrote a whopper of a check to pay for my basket. It's sturdy. I think it will hold up well so that my daughter will one day gather flowers in her garden with this basket. I like the thought of that. I like using things that I know were used by the women who came before me in my family. I like the worn places on the silver where other hands held goblets, trays, and pitchers. I like the thin edges of jewelry that have been handled by several generations of Southern women who shared my DNA. I like thinking that even if I don't make it to old age, my daughter, granddaughter, or maybe even a great-granddaughter will place her hands on the handle of my sweetgrass basket exactly where I place my hands to gather flowers today. It will be like holding hands with the women who have come before and after me when I am gone to glory.

That's it. That's all I like about yard work: the hat, the gloves, the basket, and cutting the flowers to arrange on the porch, under the ceiling fan where it is cool. I do not like to be hot. Under no circumstances do I like to be sweaty. I don't want to be responsible for feeding or watering anything that doesn't have a heartbeat. What I have learned is that I can either rear my children or raise flowers. I can't do both. I know, I know. There are women who can do both of those jobs well. Good for them. Unfortunately, I am not one of them.

In the past twenty years, I can only recall two full days I spent working in my yard. That's all, two days—ten years apart. You know how I spent the two weeks after the two days of yard work? Itching. Scratching. Popping steroid pills. Both times I worked in my yard, I ended up with poison ivy. It's not worth it to me. You work in the yard. I'll ride by in my car, lean out my car window, and tell you what a good job you are doing while I sip on a glass of sweet tea with crushed ice and lemon. Better still, call me, and I'll swing by, bring you a pound cake, and arrange the flowers for you. I'll even wear my gardening hat with the green bow and my green toile gloves. You'll love them. I do.

A Controlled Burn

Morgan Murphy

Having worked as an executive editor at *Southern Living,* most people expect me to be a master chef, expert gardener, and decorator extraordinaire. I remind them that I was the travel editor, which meant I enjoyed other people's labor in those aforementioned fields. Before joining the magazine, I read cookbooks like works of fiction, used worn-out car parts and dead animals to decorate my bachelor pad, and cultivated only one form of plant life: mold.

Yet spending years around the most brilliant writers and photographers in the South had to rub off somehow. Judy Feagin, the grande dame of our test kitchen, convinced me to dabble in the alchemy of cooking, and her recipes were a welcome respite from my usual dinner of a can of tuna fish, lemon juice, and wheat bread. I also began to study English and Greek architecture. What Southerner doesn't like a good Corinthian column? Shoot, I'd put a column on my mailbox if I could. At last, I worked my way up to gardening.

I adore gardens. I accidentally discovered a sneak-entrance to the back of the Birmingham Botanical Gardens when I was about twelve years old. Having just read Tolkien's *The Lord of the Rings,* I thought I'd stumbled upon Middle Earth—that is, until I noticed all the plants were labeled. As a pre-teen, the Botanical Gardens became my hiding place and sanctuary. Later in life, I proposed to Mrs. Murphy in a garden. And we were married in her family's garden, designed by Frederick Law Olmsted, and saved by her mother from certain ruination. My favorite Bible verse hints of God's love of the garden, "They heard the voice of the Lord walking through the garden in the cool of the afternoon." Who doesn't adore an evening stroll in a serene botanical setting?

Our first house sat upon one-eighth of an acre, which meant I could blow leaves off my lawn with a hair dryer. It was great. I planted stuff. It lived. I rejoiced.

Still, that garden was too small for my favorite foliage. I particularly delight in Southern plants that smell like Southern women: gardenias, camellias, magnolias, and jasmine. Dogwoods and azaleas dazzle me, too. You can't grow a decent magnolia in a cramped space.

So when we found a house on an acre, I leapt at the chance to own a bigger garden where I could get a larger fix for all things green and growing. I thought, stupidly, that an acre wouldn't take that much additional time to tend. I also assumed that Mrs. Murphy enjoyed the great outdoors and would help.

Uh, wrong. Mrs. Murphy is a woman of the great indoors. We're like a modern-day version of *Green Acres.* I carry on about fresh air and wear large garden boots. Mrs. Murphy prefers the rarefied air of Saks and footwear with impractical heels.

Upon moving in we discovered that our new garden had been lost to the ravages of time. (Never a "yard" mind you. Prisoners walk in a "yard.") Great swaths of Chinese wisteria choked the trees, bushes, and even a side of the house. Confederate jasmine crept up the walls and across the attic joists. Juniper cracked the foundation. Hundreds of discarded pots and trash bags littered the lawn. Verdant green moss covered the roof. The roots of a mighty oak, half-dead from a lightning strike, encircled and crushed the home's drainage system, collapsed the driveway, and eroded a retaining wall. A small tree grew from one gutter. A flat roof harbored a forest of mushrooms. Many a critter, from rats to snakes, claimed the garage, guest cottage, and other outbuildings. Squirrels had buried acorns in the kitchen walls. The windows were bright green from the moisture and mildew. In short, the place was a disaster. Mother Nature is lovely, yes, but I prefer her on more controlled terms.

Yet in springtime, even an overgrown garden can be gorgeous. Exotic bulbs burst into view. Ornamental grasses sprang forth from the most unlikely spots. English Lenten roses and fragrant hyacinths blossomed. So before I began my quest to reclaim our new house from its bed of vines, I invited the legendary editor-in-chief of *Southern Living*, Dr. John Alex Floyd, Jr., to stroll our lot and give me his best advice on what to save.

John's signature Selma drawl and booming laugh punctuated nearly every meeting at *Southern Living* for thirty years. He boasts a PhD in horticulture, so the man can identify any herb, grass, tree, or bush by its Latin and familiar name. He's a walking encyclopedia of all things plant.

For thirty minutes we strolled my lawn in silence. He ducked beneath vines. He fingered the leaves of various bushes. He gazed upwards at the rapidly spreading branches and stooped down to examine the flowers. I was a nervous host, eager to get direction from a man who was like a father to me in so many ways.

"So, Dr. Floyd," I asked, "which plants do I keep? What should I do first?"

John paused for a long moment and looked at me over his glasses. Then he swept his arm across the outline of our property. "Maw-gahn," he said, "I'd have a controlled *BURN*." With that, he stepped into his Buick and sped off, leaving me in a tangle of weeds.

Fortunately, like many other Southerners, I'd had some experience in controlled burns. The most likely target of a controlled burn in the South is an old green creep that scares small children, a leafy calamity that harbors bugs and snakes, a botanical boogey that swallows abandoned farmhouses whole: kudzu.

In Dixie, there's a lot of kudzu to hate because the weed already covers seven million acres by the U.S. Forest Service's last count, and it's still on the move. Up poles. Over trees. Under cars. Across back roads. Around abandoned household appliances. Down into the red clay with roots that can burrow up to five feet. And into the psyche of generations of Southerners who've been confounded by the wily vine.

Kudzu, *Pueraria lobata*, was brought to America by the Japanese in 1876, and I haven't forgiven them yet. In Alabama, kudzu was scrutinized by Auburn University agronomists, who touted it as a remedy for soil erosion and a replacement for old King Cotton, a crop that had been withering since Reconstruction. What was to have been a peaceful transfer of power, however, soon became a kudzu coup. In Japan and other northerly latitudes, harsh winters had kept kudzu in check—but in the sweltering Southland, kudzu ran amok.

For years folks loved kudzu: The government paid farmers as much as eight dollars per acre to plant the verdant Medusa; kudzu clubs were founded; Miss Kudzu Queen of Greensboro, Alabama, was crowned in 1930; and in the '40s the vine became a popular feed crop for livestock.

Unfortunately, as a potent member of the bean family (*Fabaceae*), kudzu caused acute distress among our four-stomached bovine friends. An epidemic of cows plagued by that famous bloated feeling led to the invention of a lance for "popping" kudzu cattle.

But trying to eradicate kudzu from one's own yard can be even more life threatening than exploding cow flatulence. My father once attempted to kill the kudzu that was taking over our backyard. First, with red face and blistered hands, he tried to pull it up during the winter, when the vine turns brown and dries out. Mama worried he'd electrocute himself pulling it off the power lines to the house, but before March had ended, her roses were choked and the green peril threatened the Electra station wagon. It was either us or the kudzu. The roots had survived the attack, so the next winter Daddy went at it with an old Southern recipe for kudzu destruction: diesel fuel and a hoe. That failed, so he tried an ax. Then a bulldozer. Then weed killer. Nothing worked. Fortunately, I was away at camp when he escalated the fight with kudzu to Biblical proportions by plowing salt into the soil and setting fire to the lot.

The kudzu lived. We moved.

Unlike my parents, the South hasn't given up trying to wipe out kudzu. Researchers at North Carolina State University recently came up with a hybrid caterpillar-wasp bug that eats the stuff. The caterpillars are injected with wasp larvae, a little trick that increases their hunger for kudzu. Then right before the caterpillars spin a cocoon, the wasps eat the caterpillars and, soon after, fly away. Is this the best solution modern science could come up with?

I skipped the wasps and stuck to old-fashioned kudzu clearing. Like my father before me, I pulled it off trees and from under the house. I hacked it and hacked it good, along with heaps of other assorted brush, weeds, vines, and that great botanic Satan, privet. Many neighbors undoubtedly thought we were crazy—some sort of anti-nature couple, hell-bent on destroying flora and fauna of every sort. Many evenings I came inside covered in dirt, bruises, scratches, and sores. I often looked so haggard and exhausted that my wife's visiting friends and voice students mistook me for the gardener (my wide-brimmed hat, green shirt, and khaki pants added to the look). The questions they asked were often revealing, "When are Mr. and Mrs. Murphy going to plant turf?" or, "What are they doing with the yard?" Or my favorite, "Why did they cut back that pretty—*insert name of invasive, non-native shrub or plant?*"

"There's no telling, I'm just the hired help," I'd exclaim standing on my own front lawn. "Them people are just plain crazy!"

In moments like that, I often felt that the plants were winning the war and the PR battle.

But when the going gets tough, the tough get Roundup, a Craftsman chainsaw, and a weed whacker. Suitably armed,

I beat that acre into submission. And once everything was cleared and the dreaded kudzu was gone for good, I came back with a new elm, two crepe myrtles, four oaks, eleven Japanese maples, twelve tons of topsoil, twenty-seven tons of sandstone, thirty-eight rose bushes, forty-seven hydrangeas, 135 boxwoods, and thirteen thousand square feet of zoysia.

Neighbors delighted. Friends praised. Passing visitors asked if I could tend their lawns. My inner garden ego bloomed.

Then, one evening last month I happened to be walking the backyard with the dog. Glancing down, I saw it: the first leafy curl of my dreaded Japanese enemy—kudzu. Naturally, I let out a blood-curdling yell, sprang into DEFCON 6, and banished the invader. Yet I'm certain it won't be the last sprig of kudzu to pop up in the yard.

Kudzu's persistence might be irritating to some gardeners. Somehow, though, I'm comforted by the thought that when the South's last barbecue smolders and dies; when the last pickup truck sputters to a stop; when the last column falls off the last plantation house; when diners in Yazoo, Mississippi, and Eufala, Alabama, succumb to mocha-decaf-cappuccino-skim lattes—kudzu will still be there, creeping at a rate of twelve inches per day, tucking every vestige of our glorious region under a thick, green quilt.

How to Look and Sound Like a Pro in the Garden

So what if you have a black thumb? Do plants recoil from you in horror? Don't fret: here are some tips to make you look like a horticultural genius.

Never utter something so banal as "fountain" or "creek." It is a "water feature."

The space around your home isn't a *yard*. Prisoners walk in a yard. The rest of us tend to the lawn or garden.

Talk about composting, natural herbicides, and old folk remedies for what ails your plants. Then nuke 'em in the dead of night with napalm.

Learn a few Latin phrases, i.e., "Oh, the *Buxus microphylla japonica* we put in last weekend made all the difference!"

Plant things that bloom and smell: lavender, gardenias, magnolias, jasmine, roses, etc.

Don't beat yourself up when stuff croaks. You have to kill a plant at least three times to really get to know it.

Buy living plants, not cut flowers. When the flowers fade, bury the sucker out back.

Learn to love dirt. It's the backbone of any great garden.

Collect the good tools. A great spade makes the digging easier, and nothing feels more decadent than a fancy watering can.

Don waterproof shoes. Few things are more miserable than soggy sneakers caked with, er, fertilizer.

Chapter 18

You Are What You Wear

All Dressed Up

I love to get dressed up for a dinner party with friends. It makes me feel special. Feminine. Alluring. Exciting. I'm not, of course. Not a bit. Although I've been married a long time, I still miss the anticipation of date evenings, more than the actual dating, which rarely leads to anything like the fairy tales promise. (Have you read any traditional fairy tales? The witch tries to EAT Hansel and Gretel. Remember? The Grimm brothers make Stephen King look tame.)

The time a woman spends getting ready for a date is chock-full of anticipation. Most of all, I miss wondering what the first kiss will be like. I like the second right before a kiss best—the moment when you know you are about to be kissed but before you actually feel the touch of his lips. Do you know the moment I mean? Close your eyes. Concentrate. Remember?

I'm a stay-at-home mother. Much as it pains me to admit it, I look like one. I'd like to be mistaken for a glamorous movie star, a dangerous undercover agent, or even a sexy, high-priced call girl, but that is so unlikely that I snorted out loud just trying to imagine it for this chapter. I wish I could say that I grew up to be something interesting, but I did not. I grew up to be a mom, the most under-appreciated, overlooked, taken-for-granted, least glamorous profession in the world. One of my favorite humorists, Erma Bombeck, called motherhood "the second oldest profession." That says it all right there.

If I walked by you at a football game, you'd say, "I bet she's a mom." The suburban mom uniform is fairly standard issue: casual slacks, T-shirt, lightweight jacket, and expensive shoes and/or handbag. The accessories are supposed to make up for the lack of fashion-awareness in the rest of the package. The alternate mom uniform is black exercise pants or sweatpants, a T-shirt, no makeup, sneakers, and expensive sunglasses.

I didn't always look like this. I can remember when getting ready for a party took two whole hours. I'd begin with a glass of wine and a bubble bath. Sometimes, I'd put cucumbers on my eyes and indulge in a spa-produce moment in my very own bathroom. Then, I'd moisturize every inch of my body with an expensive lotion that matched my perfume—as opposed to the anti-aging, anti-dry-skin lotion I purchase by the bucket at the drugstore now. After that, I'd apply a coat of clear polish to my nails and spend another hour or so experimenting with makeup and hairstyles. Outfit and shoe selection could take another half hour, at least. I'd discard mounds of clothes near the full-length mirror in my bedroom, searching for the perfect outfit. Often, I solicited other girlfriends' opinions over the telephone. Before my children were born, I had time for all that.

Now, things are different. I have teenagers. I'm lucky if there is enough hot water for me to get all the shampoo out of my hair before it runs out. Regardless of how much time I allow for getting ready, I'm doomed to be interrupted a thousand times for pressing needs like: a call from the principal, a ride home because baseball practice ended early, or to get gum out of an American Girl doll's hair (which is important, I admit, since the hair on those dolls costs more than a handmade wig of human hair). In the middle of my spa moment, someone else in my home will need to use MY bathroom for an EMER-GENCY, because all the other bathrooms are occupied. I will have to get out of the tub, grab a towel, and stand dripping in my bedroom while one of my children uses my bathroom.

When I slip on my stockings now, I am grateful if I have remembered to shave both legs. I can no longer see my bottom half in the full-length mirror in the bedroom I share with my husband because he routinely stacks boxes of legal cases in front of it. (All the kids in our house have their own bedrooms. I do not see why I have to share. I am too old to have a roommate.) I have to peer over the boxes to see if the little black dress I bought two years ago, but have never had an opportunity to wear, still fits over my hips without breaking any indecent-exposure laws.

I was excited about this dinner party. It was a friend's birthday. She and her husband are tons of fun, and I felt pretty in that dress until my husband leaned over, halfway through dinner, and whispered in my ear that the price tags had been swinging back and forth under my right armpit during the first three courses. I wave my arms a lot when I talk, so this vision made me feel slightly sick. I wouldn't have minded so much— it was a VERY nice dress, after all—if it hadn't been marked down in red ink three times to a rock-bottom sale price that was less than I spend on a month's supply of flea medicine for the cat. To be completely honest, if it hadn't been marked down to almost nothing, I wouldn't have bought it.

I admit the shoes were a mistake, but remember, I could only see the top half of the outfit in the mirror. I tried holding one foot up at a time like a drum majorette, but I still didn't see the whole ensemble until I went to the lady's room in the restaurant. It was worse than I had feared. Instead of looking as if I had gotten dressed in a rush, I looked like a crazy woman. My eyeliner was crooked. Also, I had no idea that my hair looked like that in the back. I am blind as a bat, nearsighted enough to need a dog and a cane, and now in need of reading glasses to apply lipstick so that the red color I favor doesn't look like a knife slash above my chin. I was afraid I looked like the Joker.

I can't figure out how to use my magnifying makeup mirror and my reading glasses at the same time, so I can't say with any authority what my curly hair looks like in the back anymore. Now, I just leave it up to God. I distinctly remember nodding off for a few minutes in the car on the way to the restaurant, so maybe that explains the hair. My teenagers were out late the previous night. I can't sleep until they come in. Sadly, unlike teenagers who can sleep late the day after a party, I have to get up at the crack of dawn. I'm tired all the time. It has become a way of life again for me with teenagers just like it was when I had three children under the age of five. Back then, I walked around like a tired intern during the last twenty minutes of a twenty-four-hour shift. I guess the catnap is why my hair looked like it had been mashed flat with an iron. I hope no one thought I wore it like that on purpose.

I didn't want to wear my reading glasses to the restaurant because I think they make me look about as sexy as an insurance adjustor, so I took a gamble on the menu offerings and pointed to a blurry item that looked promising. I think I ate sheep's testicles. I can't be sure because I couldn't see the dish up close, which is just as well, now that I think about it. Why would a fancy professional chef choose to cook sheep's testicles out of all the things in the world that he could prepare? I tell you I do not know these things.

As usual, it was hard to get out the front door of my house. I felt like I was running a gauntlet of obstacles like a medieval knight. In the hall, I tilted at windmills, fought off dragons, and battled my way to the exit. As I closed the door, I threatened my children with the loss of text messaging, computer access, and other fates worse than death if they didn't complete their homework before I returned from the dinner party.

Inadvertently, in the rush to escape with my husband, I grabbed a dark-blue baseball windbreaker from the hall closet instead of my black velvet evening cloak. I considered going back to retrieve the evening jacket, a much more appropriate and flattering choice, but my husband and I agreed that re-entering the fray was not worth the risk. As a result, I had to take the valet's hand, alight from the car, and step into the restaurant with a giant Patriot head blazoned across my chest. It clashed horribly with the rhinestone buckles on my evening shoes. I tried to hold my head high and look eccentric and interesting rather than mental, as the Brits would put it, but I don't think it worked.

I looked like what I am: a suburban mom of athletes who owns a sports jacket that is ugly as sin but warm enough to keep out the wind and rain for nine endless innings. Worse, I looked like a mom pretending to be something I am not: a normal woman out for a romantic evening with her husband. The windbreaker did nothing to enhance my image. I was more than happy to hand over that jacket to the coat-check girl. I had no plans to reclaim it at the end of the evening. I planned to drink enough wine to induce a series of hot flashes guaranteed to keep me warm all night long.

About halfway through dinner, I made another trip to the powder room. It was one of many, since our host had chosen a birthday wine-trip-around-the-world with each course, which was divine but did not go well with the spandex undergarment I was wearing. I felt like a newborn puppy that needs to be taken outside every five minutes.

When I looked in the ornate mirror in the lady's room, I was shocked to realize that I'd only applied rouge to one cheek. I do remember being interrupted during the blush-application process by a skirmish between my middle child and his little sister that required my intervention before it blew up into something you'd expect to see on the India-Pakistan border. Obviously, I had forgotten to apply rouge to the other cheek after my return from the emergency diplomatic summit downstairs. My one red cheek looked as if it had been slapped. Hard.

I could see the headlines: "Judge's Wife Shows Evidence of Abuse." That would be true, in a sense. Although my husband is perfectly nice to me, I think my children are under the false impression that I work for them. Somehow, they have come to believe that they live in a very nice resort. The staff is made up of my husband and me. In their minds, we are available twenty-four hours a day, seven days a week, to chauffeur, feed, finance, and generally smooth the way for their all-important social lives. Lost or broken items? No need to try and find them or attempt to repair them. Money is no problem. The STAFF will take care of everything.

I am scheduling a staff meeting at our house. I do not know how we have come to this. I really don't. How could I, a well-educated, experienced, wily mother of three children, be reduced to a red-cheeked, windbreaker-wearing, half-dressed lunatic whose only crime is attempting to eat a fancy dinner in the company of other adults who won't complain about the entrée offerings, send furtive text messages under the table, or ask to be excused before I've even lifted my fork to begin eating? How did I allow this to happen?

I hate to tell you this, but it's not just me, you know. All of you look like what you are, too. Bankers look like bankers. Lawyers look like lawyers. Teachers look like teachers. Wait staff looks like wait staff. I can sit on a park bench, watch the crowd walk by, and name each person's profession within an acceptable margin of error for a professional polling organization. I can even do part-timers. For example, I can size up a stranger and tell you that not only is the woman a waitress, she is a model/actress/waitress. I am that good.

When an opportunity to dress up presents itself, I'm excited. It's fun to pretend to be someone else for a few hours. Is it too much to ask that moms be allowed to dress up as real people from time to time? I don't think so. For you men who don't live in mommy-world, let me give you a tip. The next time you zero in on an attractive woman at a party, who seems a little overexcited, do not assume she is high on drugs. She may be a mom who doesn't get out much. It doesn't take a lot to get us excited. If you see her hand reach out to take a glass of wine, and you read the word *PAID* stamped across the top of her knuckles, it doesn't mean what you're thinking. God does not drop pretty women in your lap like that. It means that the woman is a MOM, and she had about twenty minutes to get dressed for a night out after her son's baseball game. She did the best she could. Just so you know, it takes about a week for those PAID stamps to wash off.

Dress-Up Clues

If a woman has gone to the trouble of dressing up for a date with you, don't forget to compliment her appearance. To determine how much effort she expended, look for these clues:

If the woman is wearing more makeup than she wore on her wedding day, tell her she looks pretty. She obviously pulled out the big cover-up stick.

If she has on lipstick that matches her outfit—as opposed to Chapstick she smeared across her dry lips without looking in a mirror—she gave it some thought.

If she is wearing panty hose to spare you the sight of her spider-vein collection, you should offer her your thanks on bended knee.

If she has a fresh manicure and a pedicure, she is looking for action. Take her out to dinner. You could get lucky.

If she has a handbag that looks too small to hold anything more than a credit card and a peppermint, she wants an adventure.

If her hair is blow-dried and hair-sprayed, she is practically begging you to order her a drink with an umbrella in it.

If she left her Dollar Store reading glasses at home in order to appear more attractive to you, offer to whisper the restaurant's dessert offerings in her ear.

continued

If she suddenly appears ten pounds slimmer than yesterday, and she seems chronically short of breath, you can safely assume she's wearing a girdle.

If she smells like something you pay for by the ounce rather than the bacon she fried for breakfast, she's excited about your date.

On the other hand, if a woman answers the door sporting sweatpants, a ponytail, and no makeup, the evening is going nowhere. Trust me on this.

Invasion of the Suit Snatchers

Casual Day. Those two words denote the ruination of our civilization, the collapse of all that is good and decent in our land. The unknotting of the necktie will be the unraveling of our social threads, mark my words.

When I began working in the mail room of a local advertising company in 1987, I wore a tie and a blue blazer to work—to sort mail. Let me repeat that: I wore a necktie to deliver letters and packages. My manager wore a tie. His boss wore a tie. The CEO wore a tie, albeit plaid, every day. Men wore starched shirts and neckties to toil at offices, stump for political power, pray in churches, grieve at funerals, celebrate at weddings, feast on fancy dinners, and swill booze at cocktail parties. We wore ties and we didn't think twice about it. Verily, we looked good.

We looked good because a fine suit covers a multitude of sins. A master tailor sews a man to greatness one careful snip at a time; he can make you taller, thinner, stronger, and he can make you appear to be in control. Those golden scissors and fine fabrics work wonders. The expertly tailored suit descends directly from a knightly suit of armor, protecting its occupant from the slings, arrows, and bad coffee of the workaday world.

Pre-Casual Day, a man needed a blue blazer and a charcoal suit. That's it, unless he was Southern, in which case a seersucker suit and white bucks were mandatory.

Back then, men getting dressed in the morning paused briefly in their boxer shorts and dark socks (a hideous sight, to be sure) to contemplate a few things. Men pondered whether the occasion called for a suit or a sports coat. Gentlemen fretted about white versus tattersall shirts or belts versus braces. Socks to match the suit or the shoes? Cotton or silk handkerchief? Oh, and what tie to wear? Those were the biggest questions in the decision department.

We most certainly did not deeply consider matters of style on a daily basis. That was the point of having rules—so you didn't have to actually think while getting dressed. For instance, men knew not to wear elaborate shoes with a tuxedo. We knew not to mix stripes and checks or brown and black. In doubt? Ask your tailor. Still befuddled? Put on a white shirt and a dark suit—your tie could light up like a Vegas casino and you'd still be within the bounds of the acceptable. How quaint our old rules seem today. For today, dear friends, we men have been duped. Tricked, I tell you. Chicanery in the closet. Hucksterism on the hanger. And it all started with Casual Friday.

Oh, that Trojan horse, Casual Friday. "We'll loosen the rules for one day," thought the company managers. "We'll be hip, cool, and score some points with workers who tire of dressing up for the office," they naively thought. "Plus, it's a free perk." Those imbeciles knew not what they wrought.

Casual Friday soon turned into Laissez-Faire Monday, Takin'-out-the-Trash Tuesday, Sweatpants Wednesday, and Dude! Thursday. Men who once would have committed harakiri before wearing rubber-soled shoes to church suddenly found themselves thinking, "Well this elastic waistband sure would come in handy at lunch!" With casual attire came casual manners. Bankers and lawyers gave two-thousand-dollar suits to the Salvation Army. Tailors became as rare as fiscal discipline in Washington, D.C. Busboys and waiters looked overdressed next to their new, casual, clientele.

You know it's bad when you gaze wistfully at photos of unemployed workers from the Great Depression, and note that they're wearing suits, ties, and fedoras *in breadlines.*

Yet some men, intent on looking presentable, try to look casual and smartly dressed at the same time. That requires something most men do not inherently possess: a sense of fashion.

Fashion, traditionally, was something your girlfriend, wife, or teenage daughter spent time contemplating. Fashion takes creativity. It takes "keeping up." It takes financial resources and tireless shopping. Fashion requires thought, and indeed spurs a self-questioning among femininity that heretofore men scarcely recognized: "What handbag should I tote to the office?" "Is this event cocktail or full-length?" "Is this belt too much?" "Are these shoes too suggestive?" "Do these jeans make me look fat?"

It was one thing when your wife/sister/whatever asked you those questions. It's altogether another situation when, as a man, you find yourself asking, "Does this sweater make me look paunchy?" Good Lord.

Great chieftains of commerce, who once donned gray flannel without a second thought, now spend hours upon agonizing hours matching button-downs to crew necks. Titans of capitalism pour over clothing catalogs as they once did financial reports. Men of all stripes now swoon when someone says, "I like your outfit today." Think of the wasted time, the squandered resources, and the ridiculous preoccupation with being in style.

Who, as men, do we have to blame for this? (Because, of course, we men need someone to blame.) I have a suspicion: I believe it was the women's fashion industry that drove us to this. Just another random conspiracy theory from a disgruntled Southern male? Nay, nay. I have some experience with the women's fashion industry, having started my magazine career at *Harper's Bazaar.* That's right—I was one man among seventy-five female editorial staffers. A sole Y in a torrent of Xs, doing the backstroke in a pool of estrogen.

I soon learned a lot about women by working at *Harper's Bazaar*. I divined that if a way to a man's heart is through his stomach, a way to a woman's soul is through her soles. Eyes aren't the clue to a woman's passions; her wildly expensive handbag gives greater insight. A stylish haircut offers more therapy than Freud could ever conjure on a couch. And yes, chocolate does cure what ails you. As I really do adore women, I devoured these tips like an Allied spy in Stalin's map room.

Something more insidious caught my attention as well. I call it "fashion churn." Magazines and the fashion industry instruct a woman to perpetually update and reinvent her wardrobe, her makeup, her accessories, and her haircut. This churn, not surprisingly, is good for the sales of Bobby Brown, Revlon, Chanel, et al. To illustrate: the worst insult my grandmother ever received was from her arch-nemesis in Andalusia, a woman so vicious and vile that I can only reveal her initials to you: Anne Greer. Anyway, Mrs. Greer spotted grandmother at church one Sunday and said, "Oh, Helen, I just *always* love that hat," referring to my grandmother's favorite headpiece. Grandmother never wore it again.

My grandfather, by contrast, wore the same hat, every day, for thirty years. Today, most men don't gasp with horror if they walk into a party and see other men wearing a black tuxedo with a white wing collar. We don't gossip about other fellows who wear the same suit twice or even three times a week. The fact that your overcoat survived seven presidential administrations can be a pleasant topic of conversation. I own three pairs of dress shoes. Three.

Being the old-fashioned sort, I recently splurged on a gray chalk-stripe suit. Not just any suit: a really smart number with hand-stitched lapels; sleeve buttons that truly work; custom silk lining; pockets for every fountain pen, wallet, and mobile phone imaginable; and a double set of trousers. The tailor, from a venerable Savile Row firm that dates back to 1689 (that's right—older than the United States) charged me seven hundred pounds, which exceeded the sales price of my first car. The price (about twelve hundred U.S.) was so outrageous, so hideously expensive and decadent, that I debated for about six months over whether to buy it. It was not until the seat of the pants on my existing gray suit became so shiny I could comb my hair in them, that I finally relented and bought the boring gray English duds. Justification time: I generally keep a suit at least ten years and wear it a minimum of once a week. (Bear with me here, I'm going to delve into some mathematics.) That works out to 520 uses for that twelve hundred dollar suit, or $2.31 per occasion. I agonized for six months over $2.31.

How unfair, by contrast, stands the average woman's purchase. Buy a bridesmaid's gown; wear it once (maybe twice). Purchase a suit; don it for a season—maybe two—for a total of a dozen wears. Want a divorce? Suggest to your wife she needs but three pair of shoes.

So you would think, then, that women's clothing would be less expensive given these social constraints. Ha. Let this be a warning to you, Jimmy Choo. I'm not a violent man, but if I ever find you, I'm going to beat you with your own high heels. I'd love to clock Mr. Hermès with his exquisitely molded handbags. There will be fisticuffs if Oscar de la Renta shows his face in Birmingham.

The women's fashion industry, having thoroughly bilked their prey into spending zillions of dollars, have now turned to men. They insist we need outfits for Casual Day, made by stylish designers (not our musty old tailors) and modeled by androgens in tight underdrawers. They insist that the old rules are gone and fashion is in command, that we need new clothes, new shoes, new fragrances, and this year's style.

Well I say no. Be a man, men, and resist this tyranny of the needle-and-thread set. Your cravat is not a noose—it is a life-rope to liberty. Embrace your inner dull. Don a suit. Shine your shoes. Prepare for battle.

The fashionistas are coming, and they want your tie.

Fashion Disasters

Pajamas in public. Unless you're Persian or Urdu, you have no business wearing pajamas beyond the foot of your driveway.

Messages on your butt. Recently, on a Delta flight to D.C., a large woman sat next to me wearing a pink outfit with the word *SEXY* emblazoned in rhinestones on her posterior. Two words: false advertising.

Athletic apparel outside of a gym: sneakers in Paris, sweatpants at the grocery store, baseball caps *everywhere*. Unless you look athletic or are in the midst of some sort of exercise or competitive sport, wear real clothing.

Latex, spandex, Velcro, Lycra, vinyl, and pleather—a man shouldn't wear man-made fabric.

Q & A with Melinda & Morgan

1. **How much of this book is based on your own experiences with your significant others? Or at least, how much are you willing to admit to? How do they feel about the book?**

Melinda: *All the people in my essays are real people. In my first book, I didn't call them by their real names. Then I realized that was silly. My humor is always at my expense, no one else's, so my husband, friends, and children always come out smelling like a rose, no matter how ridiculous I look. I find it is better to ask forgiveness later—after those people see their names in print—rather than permission first, which can be tricky. All my friends have a good sense of humor. Otherwise, we would not be friends for long. My children would rather not appear in my books at all, of course, but I don't care one bit. I am a mean mama.*

Morgan: *My significant other, Mrs. Murphy, maintains a robust sense of humor. We seldom argue and rarely even disagree. But that's boring, right? So I used a lot of material from past, less successful relationships.*

2. **How did you two put this book together, since Melinda had most of her essays written when Morgan came on board?**

Melinda: *This project came together like every other project between a man and a woman comes together. I had an idea. I plotted. I talked Morgan into doing what I wanted. At first, I think he just wanted to shut me up and make me happy. In the end, he actually enjoyed himself, just like I told him he would. It's an old story.*

Morgan: *I did as I was told.*

3. Did the two of you run into any problematic subjects when writing this book?

Melinda: *Not really. I am the boss. Usually, Morgan does what I want. Almost always, we agreed about where we were going in the book. Once or twice, I gave in gracefully. Morgan is brilliant. If he puts up a fuss about something, he is usually right.*

Morgan: *Is this a trick question? Everything Melinda did was just FINE. Remember, I have to tour with this woman, so I'm erring on the side of caution here.*

4. Were you surprised by any of your coauthor's essays on a particular subject? Enlightened? Enraged?

Melinda: *I am always entertained by Morgan's take on any subject—even when he's totally misguided and wrong.*

Morgan: *Melinda is one of the funniest people I know. Do not read her essays while sipping on anything. I literally did a "spit take" as we used to say in the theatre and shot bourbon right up my nose while reading her essay, "All Dressed Up". Even when she says something totally at odds with the universe and altogether wrong, you can't help but laugh.*

5. Do you think any of the gender-specific behaviors/ attitudes in *I Love You—Now Hush* are specific to the South?

Melinda: *Men will be men, and women will love or hate those men, depending upon their mood, the world over, until the earth stops spinning. In the South, there are added cultural complexities that make the interaction between the sexes particularly combustible. When I first started writing about the South, I thought Southern women would be my only audience. I was wrong. Women—and men—from all over the country are*

interested in reading about Southerners. The themes are univer-
sal. The Southern part is just an angle.

Morgan: *Southern women are a totally different species.
Period. When you see them wandering the streets of some foreign city, such as New York or Philadelphia, they immediately
stand out. Sure, the hair and makeup differences are acute. But
you'll also notice differences in subtle ways, such as the way
they flirt with everyone and call titans of capitalism "honey" or
"sugar." So while much of the book applies to all women (I'm
sure there's a dame in some third world country saying, "No
dear, don't bother yourself with getting water from the well. I'll
carry it on my head for the next three miles. That's fine."), it really was written for the women I know best—Southern women.*

**6. Do you feel like your essays exemplify the male
and female stereotypes accepted in today's society? Do
either of you feel you stepped out of the stereotype for
your gender?**

Melinda: *In many ways, Morgan and I are fairly stereo-
typical representatives of our people, yet our culture here in
the South encourages us to be something more. Good manners
down here—even in the twenty-first century—require men to be
gentlemen and women to be ladies. Morgan really is a gentleman. He lives up to the hype. I have a little more trouble with
my role as a Southern "lady." I'm a little bit suspicious about
that noun. However, I cannot deny that if anyone were to say
to me that I am NOT a lady, I would be as mortally offended as
Scarlett O'Hara. In other words, there is no pleasing me. Southern women, like all women, are more than a stereotype, and one
underestimates them at one's peril. What makes this book interesting is the inherent conflict between my XX and Morgan's
XY chromosomes. The exaggeration of those differences—which
we do well in the South—makes for good theater.*

Morgan: *Mark Twain said that the root of all humor is*

sorrow. There's truth in that, especially when it comes to stereotypes. I think stereotypes can be funny because we get a little tired of them and sometimes feel hemmed in. Speaking personally, Mrs. Murphy and I do often fall into stereotypes. I change the oil in the car; she does the dishes. I fix leaky pipes; she mends the curtains. In that way, our marriage would cause Gloria Steinem, et. al., to have strokes. But then again, we both defy stereotypes as well. I like to cook bread and garden. Our main toilet line busted and Mrs. Murphy fixed it. So I think of stereotypes like a church pew—it's comfortable to sit in the same pew, week after week, and hopefully that gives you the inner peace to explore new emotional boundaries and think a bit past your limit.

7. Do you think this book will help men and women understand each other better?

Melinda: *Good grief, no. This isn't a self-help book. This is just for fun. If reading it helps some man or woman accidentally, of course, I guess that's a good thing . . . but we're not offering any money-back guarantees.*

Morgan: *Sure. I got some good tips from Melinda's chapter on romance. I literally thought, "Boy, I need to remember that tip," on a few of them.*

8. What was the worst part of working with a coauthor? The best?

Melinda: *The worst part about having a coauthor is that you have to halve the profits. The best part is that you have somebody to whine to while you are writing the book who really, really understands.*

Morgan: *Working with Melinda was a complete delight. It was a blast to work with another writer who is funny and dedi-*

cated to her readers. There is no "worst part."

9. What did you discover about each other during the process of writing this book?

Melinda: *I discovered that Morgan is one of the few people in the world who makes me laugh out loud and that he is the only person in the world with whom I could have written this book. It would not have worked with anyone else.*

Morgan: *I didn't expect Melinda to be a vodka drinker. Or a milk chocolate person. I (wrongly) would have pegged her as a toddy-and-finger-sandwiches lady.*

10. Are either of you writing anything now?

Melinda: *Writers are always writing. Just this week, I began mentally composing an essay in church when the woman ahead of me in the choir loft told me the purse that was bumping me in the leg was from her mother's trousseau, circa 1926. I did not hear one word of the sermon. Occupational hazard.*

Morgan: *I've just finished a drive to all forty-eight continental states in a 1958 Cadillac—a car that came new with four cigar lighters, six drinking tumblers, and no seat belts. Driving a car like that in the world today made for some wild stories I'm eager to share.*

978-0-89587-329-3
$14.95 paperback

www.blairpub.com

*"Reading Melinda Rainey
Thompson's SWAG is
like sitting on Granny's
porch swing eating a
piece of pound cake with
a sleeping cat wrapped
around your ankles.
You feel full, warm, and,
most of all, grateful to
be a Southerner."*

—Celia Rivenbark,
author of *We're Just Like
You, Only Prettier*

Excerpt from *SWAG: Southern
Women Aging Gracefully*

Ten Ways To Know if
You're a SWAG:

1. You feel the urge to bake a pound cake after reading the obituaries.

2. You have had professional photographs made of your children barefoot and dressed in their Sunday clothes.

3. You'd rather have a fight with your husband than with your best friend.

4. You have stolen magnolia leaves, or you know someone who has.

5. You have monogrammed the middle of your shower curtain.

6. You could live without Yankees who equate your accent with a low IQ.

7. You know better than to eat the potato salad at a family reunion.

8. You are socially conditioned to believe that tanned fat looks better than white fat.

9. Your children hide their Easter baskets and Valentine's Day candy from you just in case you have a dieting lapse.

10. You believe that cocktail dresses do not double as church clothes.

Excerpt from *The SWAG Life*

Mailing Mama

You might think nothing interesting has happened at the post office since Miss Eudora Welty wrote about it, but you'd be wrong. Just this week, I was standing in line at the post office, minding my own business, when I overheard the customer in front of me describe the contents of the package she was mailing.

"No, it isn't fragile or hazardous," she reassured the postmistress, who is required by law to ask those sorts of questions, you know.

Then she added, voluntarily, of her own free will, as if she wasn't the least little bit ashamed to say this in front of God and everyone in line at the post office: "It's the cremated remains of my mother."

. . . That's right. There's no need to reread that paragraph. You read it correctly. That woman was mailing her mother's ashes to her sister in a town an hour's drive away, and she didn't seem a bit squeamish about it. Carrying her dead mother's ashes into the post office like a mail order of pistachio nuts didn't strike this woman as unseemly, freakish, or horribly inappropriate at all. I was getting nauseous just standing behind her in line, but she seemed completely calm about the whole shebang. . . .

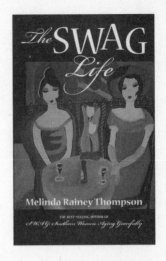

978-0-89587-351-4
$14.95 paperback

www.blairpub.com

"Thompson . . . has a knack for finding the Southern heart in ordinary life."

—*The Commercial Appeal*, Memphis

"The author definitely hits a nerve—and tickles the funny bone—with this essay collection."

—December 2006 issue of *Southern Living*

Photo by Brit Huckabay

Melinda Rainey Thompson will always be "from" the small town of Greenville, Alabama, even though she has lived in Birmingham for the past twenty-eight years. She has an undergraduate degree from Tulane University, where she was a Kappa Kappa Gamma, and an MA in English from the University of Alabama at Birmingham. She was a member of Birmingham-Southern College's English faculty from 1988 to 1994, where she taught Morgan Murphy, coauthor of *I Love You—Now Hush*. In August 1999, Melinda began writing and publishing *The SWAG Letter*, which continued for the next four years. Her first book, *SWAG: Southern Women Aging Gracefully*, was published in 2006, and was on the SIBA bestseller list for seventeen weeks in a row. Her second book, *The SWAG Life*, was published in 2007.

Melinda is married to Bill Thompson, the presiding judge of the Alabama Court of Civil Appeals. They have three children (Warner, Nat, and Lily) and a cat whose IQ matches its paw count.

Morgan Murphy is the president and founder of Motorpool.com, the world's first online social network of collector car enthusiasts.

Prior to founding Motorpool.com, Murphy served as an executive editor, travel editor, food critic, and national spokesperson for *Southern Living*. Under his leadership the magazine frequently garnered awards such as the coveted Society of American Travel Writer's Gold Award for Best Travel Coverage.

Murphy started his magazine career at *Vanity Fair*. He then joined *Forbes* magazine as a reporter. He has contributed to *Esquire*, National Public Radio, *Garden Design*, *Harper's Bazaar*, and *The New York Post*.

Murphy holds degrees from the University of Oxford and Birmingham-Southern College. Following a long family tradition of military service, he is a lieutenant commander in the United States Navy and has served the nation on four continents. His decorations include the Navy Achievement Medal, National Defense Service Medal, Global War on Terrorism

Medal, the Overseas Service Ribbon, and the Outstanding Volunteer Service Medal.

His wife, Amy, is an accomplished opera singer. The pair met while singing Gilbert and Sullivan with Skitch Henderson and the New York Pops at Carnegie Hall. The Murphys live in Birmingham and have a Springer Spaniel named Gilbert and a West Highland Terrier named Guinevere.